SO YOU THINK YOU KNOW THE DA VINCI CODE?

Clive Gifford

a division of Hodder Headline Limited

© Copyright Hodder Children's Books 2005

Published in Great Britain in 2005
by Hodder Children's Books

Editor: Vic Parker
Design by Fiona Webb
Cover design: Hodder Children's Books

The right of Clive Gifford to be identified as the author of the work
has been asserted by him in accordance with the Copyright,
Designs and Patents Act 1988.

10 9 8 7 6 5 4 3 2 1

ISBN: 034091730X

Printed by Bookmarque Ltd, Croydon, Surrey

The paper and board used in this paperback by
Hodder Children's Books are natural recyclable products made from
wood grown in sustainable forests. The manufacturing processes
conform to the environmental regulations of the country of origin.

Hodder Children's Books
a division of Hodder Headline Limited
338 Euston Road
London NW1 3BH

CONTENTS

Questions

Answers

INTRODUCTION

So you think you know *The Da Vinci Code*?
You reckon you can recall all the symbolism,
ciphers and codes in the search for true meaning
of the Holy Grail? You can remember all the
machinations and manoeuvres that take place as
the characters race to discover the Grail's long-lost
location? This book contains over 1,000 questions
which will seriously test your knowledge of Dan
Brown's blockbusting tale, and his three other
best-selling thrillers: *Angels and Demons,
Deception Point,* and *Digital Fortress.*

ABOUT THE AUTHOR

Clive Gifford is an award-winning author of more
than 80 books for children and adults including
*The Water Puppets, Espionage and Disinformation,
The Arms Trade* and *Space Exploration.* Other titles
he has written in Hodder's *So You Think You Know*
series of quiz books include: *The Simpsons,
The Lord of the Rings, Roald Dahl, Premier League
Football* and *Dr Who.* Clive can be contacted via his
website: http://www.clivegifford.co.uk.

EASY
ACCESS QUIZ

1. *The Da Vinci Code* begins with a murder in which museum?

2. What is the name of the academic caught up in the quest for the code to unlock the secret of the Holy Grail?

3. Who is the granddaughter of Jacques Saunière?

4. Which knight of the realm is actively involved in the search for the Grail?

5. In *Deception Point*, NASA claim to have discovered a giant meteorite from space – in which polar region?

6. Which murderous character in *The Da Vinci Code* is an albino?

7. What nationality is Robert Langdon?

8. In *Digital Fortress*, the assassin, Hulohot, lacks which of the five human senses?

9. In *Deception Point*, what is the name of the marine scientist who has his own weekly TV show and develops feelings for Rachel Sexton?

10. In *Angels and Demons*, who survives a fall out of a helicopter into the River Tiber?

11. What accent does the Teacher speak with?

12. In which Dan Brown book do you find a Delta Force team hunting down civilian scientists including Michael Tolland and Corky Marlinson?

13. In which city is Jacques Saunière murdered?

14. In *Deception Point*, what is the name of the US President?

15. What conservative Catholic sect believes in corporal mortification?

16. In *Digital Fortress*, what is the Star Wars-inspired nickname of the man who built Gauntlet?

17. Saunière constructed a device to store secret information. What does Sophie call this device?

18. In *Deception Point*, NASA's central headquarters are located in which US city?

19. Sir Leigh Teabing lives near which famous French palace?

20. What is the name of the policeman in charge of the investigation into Saunière's murder?

21. At which university does Robert Langdon teach?

22. In *Digital Fortress*, what is the name of the language professor who is Susan Fletcher's lover?

23. At the start of *The Da Vinci Code*, Robert Langdon is in which city?

24. In *Angels and Demons*, what is the name of Leonardo Vetra's daughter?

25. According to Robert Langdon, which famous escapologist was a Freemason?

26. In *Deception Point*, the carpet of the Oval Office in the White House is adorned with a bird holding an olive branch and some arrows. What type of bird is it?

27. In *Angels and Demons*, which place is described as the smallest country in the world: San Marino, Vatican City or Andorra?

28. Silas wears his cilice belt on which leg?

29. In *Deception Point*, which female character fell through ice when aged seven and so has harboured a fear of ice ever since?

30. In *Angels and Demons*, Robert Langdon finds a bird of peace sculpted at the top of the obelisk in the Fountain of the Four Rivers. What bird is this?

31. What is the meaning of the French word, 'Sangreal'?

32. Whose alter ego was the Teacher?

33. In *Angels and Demons*, Leonardo Vetra is branded with which word?

34. In *Deception Point*, the meteorite is dropped into which ocean to dispose of it?

35. Opus Dei's world headquarters are found in which city?

36. In *Deception Point*, what is the name of the US senator running for president?

37. Who tells Saunière that he has murdered the sénéchaux?

38. In *Digital Fortress*, how does Becker escape from the airport: on foot, on a moped, in a taxi or on a bus?

39. In *The Da Vinci Code*, in which city did Langdon last see Vittoria?

40. Which 32-year-old police officer accompanies Langdon throughout much of *The Da Vinci Code*?

41. In *Digital Fortress*, who did Rocio give Tankado's ring to: a punk, a skinhead or a Rastafarian?

42. What is the name of Sir Leigh Teabing's manservant?

43. In *Angels and Demons*, the antimatter has been transported from Geneva to which city?

44. Which famous computer entrepreneur had loaned the Codex Leicester to the Fogg Museum at Harvard?

45. Langdon's first guess at the location of the knight's tomb was which famous media thoroughfare in London?

46. Who threatened to drop and smash the cryptex, if Silas did not release Sophie Neveu?

47. Which law enforcement official returned the gold and diamond ring to Bishop Aringarosa?

48. In *Digital Fortress*, in which continent was the director of the NSA whilst the story unfolded?

49. In *Angels and Demons*, Cardinal Guidera was from which Spanish city?

50. Which pioneer of animation does Langdon cite as frequently retelling the story of the Holy Grail in his movies?

CRYPTIC AND MYSTIC

1. Teabing tells Sophie that Mary Magdalene was married to whom?

2. Sophie and Langdon bought train tickets out of Paris to which destination?

3. Who drove the taxi cab through Paris, after the cab driver was removed at gunpoint?

4. How many rounds did Silas's handgun hold?

5. What is the name of the angel found in the painting, *Madonna of the Rocks*: Uriel, Gabriel, Ariel or Pariel?

6. What is the name of the spiked belt Silas wears?

7. In *Angels and Demons*, the battery timer connected to the antimatter trap has been set for a countdown of how long: 6 hours, 12 hours, 24 hours or 48 hours?

8. How many pools circle the new entrance to the Louvre museum, La Pyramide?

9. One of the oldest ever ciphers is mentioned in the verse found on the rosewood box. Its name begins with the letter A. What is it?

10. Into what London building does the Teacher enter, shortly after his last meeting with Rémy Legaludec?

11. In *Digital Fortress*, what nationality was the first tourist to Ensei Tankado's body?

12. Bishop Aringarosa flew across the Atlantic with which airline?

13. In *Digital Fortress*, what is the name given to the highest level of security in the USA?

14. The Uffizi Gallery is in which Italian city?

15. According to *Angels and Demons*, what is the obelisk in St Peter's Square topped by: a golden orb, a marble angel pointing west or an iron cross?

16. In *Deception Point*, how long is the biggest fossil found in the meteorite: 3 cm, 12 cm, 26 cm or 60 cm?

17. Whose musical compositions did Langdon not cite as being structured according to PHI: Debussy's, Mozart's, Delius's or Schubert's?

18. In *Digital Fortress*, Susan Fletcher has a two-line coded fax taped next to her keyboard. Who sent it?

19. Lieutenant Collet examined a rental car parked close to the Château Villette. Whose was it?

20. In *Digital Fortress*, NDAKOTA turned out to be an anagram of what?

21. In *Deception Point*, Sexton met with a shady campaign financier in the car park of which building: the Mayflower Hotel, the US Senate Building, the Purdue Hotel or the Washington Monument?

22. In *Digital Fortress*, what item did Becker use to trip Hulohot and make him fall down the tower's steps?

23. In *Deception Point*, the waters around Tolland's ship are inhabited with which type of shark?

24. Who suffers from claustrophobia: Sir Leigh Teabing, Sophie Neveu, Silas or Robert Langdon?

25. What is the last letter of the Hebrew alphabet: Th, Sh or Tz?

26. In *Deception Point*, Wailee Ming's body was first spotted by which scientific instrument: a PODS satellite, ground-penetrating radar, underwater sonar or a thermal imager?

27. In *Digital Fortress*, Susan Fletcher discovers emails addressed to NDAKOTA on whose computer terminal?

28. In *Deception Point*, which White House insider sent an email to Gabrielle Ashe, asking her for a meeting at the East Appointment Gate?

29. In *Angels and Demons*, approximately how many members do the Masons have: 450,000, 800,000, 1.5 million or 5 million?

30. What is the recommended length of time for followers of The Way to wear a cilice each day?

31. Sir Leigh Teabing studied at which English university?

32. In *Deception Point*, who was Jim Samiljan: a member of the NASA team in the Arctic, a fake name Rachel Sexton gave Delta Force or the pilot of the Coast Guard helicopter?

33. Which city was founded by the Merovingians: Florence, Rome, Rouen or Paris?

34. What is the name for the theory that life was seeded on Earth from another planet: Panspermia, Disapora or Terrasymbiosis?

35. In *The Da Vinci Code*, who aims a gun at a taxi cab driver while they escape from Paris?

36. In *Deception Point*, what is the full name of the device called PODS, which is used to measure the polar ice cap?

37. In *Angels and Demons*, who conducts the search for the antimatter: the CIA, CERN's own security or the Swiss Guards?

38. Robert Langdon and Sophie Neveu left the Depository Bank of Zurich in what sort of vehicle?

39. In *Digital Fortress*, Becker is searching for a punk girl with a pendant in one ear shaped like which of the following: a cross, a human skull or an eagle?

40. Who owns the Château Villette: Sir Leigh Teabing, Jacques Saunière or the Vatican?

41. In *Angels and Demons*, can you name the last character to arrive in Vatican City in the Pope's helicopter?

42. What shape was the divan in front of the *Mona Lisa*: square, triangular, octagonal or hexagonal?

43. In *Angels and Demons*, Gunter Glick had reported for which publication before joining the BBC?

44. In *Deception Point*, what type of airliner was modified to make the two *Air Force One*s?

45. Once in a lecture, Langdon showed a modern building in New York which had been designed using the Divine Proportion number. Which building was this?

46. What metal alloy was found in a thin strip across the floor of the Church of Saint-Sulpice?

47. Who founded Opus Dei: Bishop Aringarosa, Josemaría Escrivá or Manuel Tabal?

48. At whose residence did Sophie and Langdon have their first drink since escaping the French police at the Louvre?

49. The bank's armoured car had a device which gave out its position. What was the device called?

50. Who wielded a candle-holder to smash the floor of a Parisian church, looking for the Priory keystone?

QUIZ 2

1. What colour is the second cryptex, hidden inside the first?

2. Who wet himself when held at gunpoint inside Temple Church?

3. According to *Angels and Demons*, a falling body is slowed by approximately 20% by how many square yards of drag: one, seven or 15?

4. In *The Da Vinci Code*, whose pastime was mimicking the works of Fabergé and other famous craftsmen?

5. In *Digital Fortress*, what nationality was Hulohot?

6. How many winged boys stand at the foot of Sir Isaac Newton's tomb?

7.   In *Digital Fortress*, Rocio says that the girl to whom she gave Tankado's ring was wearing a T-shirt with a flag on it – which country's flag?

8.   At the end of *Deception Point*, who commands the disposal of the meteorite in the ocean?

9.   Who stabbed his own father in the back and left home at the age of seven?

10. Whose name was featured in the last line of the message Saunière wrote on the floor with a watermark stylus?

11. In the 16th Century, which astronomer and scientist was the most famous member of the Illuminati?

12. How many years had Silas spent in jail before managing to escape?

13. In *Deception Point*, who was to meet with William Pickering at the FDR Memorial in Washington?

14. What were the deposit boxes in the Depository Bank of Zurich identified individually by: RFID chips, barcodes, electronic tags or UV light-sensitive panels?

15. Which of the following names has Venus the star and Venus the goddess not been known as: Ishtar, the Pole, the Eastern Star or Astarte?

16. The miniature pyramid at the Louvre was how many feet high?

17. In *Angels and Demons*, what language was exclusively spoken at CERN?

18. Who checked Teabing's speed dial option on his phone to discover he had placed a call to an airfield: Silas, Bishop Aringarosa, the French police or Langdon?

19. What is the name of Sophie Neveu's grandmother?

20. In *Digital Fortress*, what was the first name of Trevor Strathmore's wife?

21. What did Langdon find in his jacket's left pocket which proved that he was a police suspect?

22. In *Digital Fortress*, who surprised Chad and Midge in the director's office by returning from abroad?

23. The verse on the wooden rose from Saunière's cryptex box was written in which language?

24. When Langdon, Sophie and Teabing were deciphering the word 'Baphomet', which five-letter word did they arrive at, beginning with the letter S?

25. Who was injured by the door of the bank's armoured car exploding outwards?

26. In *Angels and Demons*, what was the name of the brand with which Camerlengo Ventresca branded himself?

27. In *Digital Fortress*, David Becker talked to a male punk, seeking out information about Megan. What was the punk's name? (It is also the name of a record label.)

28. In *Angels and Demons*, who had arranged for the Hassassin to murder the four cardinals?

29. Jacques Saunière once told his granddaughter that a certain astronomical word contained 92 other English words. What is this word?

30. In *Deception Point*, what was the puritan nickname of the head of the NRO?

31. The painting *Madonna of the Rocks* was originally intended to be placed in a church in which Italian city?

32. In *Angels and Demons*, whose nickname was König or King?

33. In *Deception Point*, what does the acronym 'EOS' stand for?

34. Which American institution does Sophie Neveu urge Langdon to telephone, in order that he reaches an answerphone message from herself?

35. In *Deception Point*, what was the name of Tolland's research ship?

36. According to *The Da Vinci Code*, two families are direct descendants of the Merovingians. One of the families has a single-word surname beginning with the letter P. What is it?

37. Which Shakespeare play had Teabing performed in during his student days with his robe open and his manhood on display?

38. In *Deception Point*, what was 'the Kiowa Warrior' a nickname for: William Pickering, a Delta Force helicopter or the name of Tolland's research submarine?

39. In *The Da Vinci Code*, who performed a foldover of the Atbash Cipher to make it easier to use?

40. Can you recall the name of either of the pillars found at Rosslyn Chapel?

41. In *Digital Fortress*, whose Skypager revealed to Susan Fletcher the details of the termination of Tankado, Cloucharde and David Becker?

42. How was Fache rumoured to have lost a lot of money: gambling, spending lavishly on a mistress or dabbling in technology stocks?

43. In *Digital Fortress*, what phrase did the inscription on Tankado's ring spell in English?

44. Which media organisation had flown Langdon to Teabing's French estate for a programme?

45. In *Angels and Demons*, a sand-grain-sized sample of antimatter was believed to hold the same amount of energy as how many tonnes of rocket-fuel: 2 tonnes, 20 tonnes or 200 tonnes?

46. In *Digital Fortress*, who offered 50,000 pesetas for a moped ridden by an Italian boy?

47. In *Deception Point*, who was the first to be hit by a bullet on the *Goya*: Tolland, Corky or Sexton?

48. Which one of the following is not one of the Louvre's three most famous artworks: the *Mona Lisa*, the *Venus de Milo*, *The Last Supper* or *Winged Victory*?

49. In *Angels and Demons*, what is the four-letter acronym of the world's largest laboratory?

50. Can you name two of the figures found in the painting, *Madonna of the Rocks*?

QUIZ 3

1. Saunière told Silas that the keystone was hidden inside which French church?

2. Who was the author of *The Art of the Illuminati*?

3. According to Teabing, which Roman emperor financed a new Bible which did not include many mentions of Jesus's human traits: Julius Caesar, Augustine or Constantine?

4. In *Digital Fortress*, who ate tofu and regularly drank from a large container of olive oil?

5. Who is the first person in *The Da Vinci Code* to light and smoke a cigarette?

6.   In *Digital Fortress*, how many thousand dollars was David Becker paid to fly to Spain?

7.   In *Deception Point*, what was the name of the Holland-class submarine that picked up Rachel, Corky and Tolland?

8.   In *The Da Vinci Code*, which religious leader flew across the Atlantic wearing a cassock?

9.   In *Deception Point*, who swapped Senator Sexton's envelopes moments before he began his press conference?

10. What was the first name of Teabing's pilot: Robert, Rémy, Richard or Rennie?

11. In *Deception Point*, as Corky Marlinson made for the Crestliner speedboat, which part of him was injured?

12. How many wine glasses are featured in the painting of *The Last Supper*?

13. Who commanded the French police at the Depository Bank of Zurich, whilst Captain Fache attempted to obtain a search warrant?

14. In what month had Bishop Aringarosa previously met the Church's hierarchy in Italy?

15. In *Digital Fortress*, how many hours had TRANSLTR been running by the time Midge and Chad discovered it was working on just one code?

16. What relation was the young verger at Rosslyn Chapel to Sophie Neveu?

17. In *Digital Fortress*, how many thousands of employees does the National Security Agency have?

18. Which artist, other than Da Vinci, had a painting in the Salle des Etats and was a member of the Priory?

19. Who had helped bring together the largest collection of goddess art in the world?

20. According to *Deception Point*, the NRO had 57 of which unmanned reconnaissance aircraft?

21. What kind of transport did Sophie and Langdon take through a notorious red-light district of Paris?

22. In *Deception Point*, which of the scientists brought in by President Herney was the first to be killed by Delta Force?

23. When Silas was in prison in Andorra, which natural event allowed him to escape?

24. According to Marie Chauvel, to what country did the Priory always intend to move the Holy Grail?

25. The depressions in Sophie's grandfather's key were of what geometric shape?

26. When Sophie was in her early twenties, she had discovered a secret door at her grandfather's house. What was it hidden by: a painting, an engraving, a tapestry or a false wooden panel?

27. In *Deception Point*, who remarks that wearing the Mark IX suit is like wearing a giant condom?

28. In *Angels and Demons*, who had secretly met with Leonardo Vetra a month before plotting Vetra's death?

29. In *Deception Point*, the only permanent piece of furniture in the White House is the bed in which bedroom?

30. By what pictogram name was the god Isis also known: Amona, Vinci, L'Isa or Sion?

31. Sophie claimed her SmartCar could travel how many kilometres per litre of fuel?

32. The Research Institute in Systematic Theology was based in which British educational institution?

33. What goddess figure could be found on the mantelpiece of Teabing's château: an Egyptian goddess, a pagan goddess, or an Ancient Greek goddess?

34. What colour were the crosses on the white tunics of the Knights Templar?

35. What is Bishop Aringarosa's first name?

36. Paris's Jardins des Tuileries were once: a clay pit, a giant open sewer, or the site of the Knights Templar headquarters?

37. The men in Saunière's grotto who performed an ancient ritual wore masks and tunics of what colour?

38. What device did Silas use to administer a beating to his back?

39. What does Neveu believe the 'PS' in her grandfather's message stands for?

40. Edouard Desrochers was the Senior Archivist at which library?

41. In *Deception Point*, when the three scientists and Rachel Sexton went out on the ice, who led?

42. Who acts as a cajoler to try to force Langdon to admit to the murder of Jacques Saunière?

43. In *Deception Point*, what was Sedgewick Sexton's real first name: Lawrence, Jack, William or Thomas?

44. What is the name of the Pope's summer residence?

45. In *Digital Fortress*, the NSA cryptographers' haunt, nicknamed the Playpen, was what number Node?

46. In *Angels and Demons*, how old was Vittoria when she was adopted by Leonardo Vetra: eight, nine, 10 or 11 years old?

47. What was the name of the Bio Entanglement Physicist whom Langdon falls for in *Angels and Demons*?

48. How many years ago did Sophie and her grandfather fall out?

49. What is the name of the gallery in which the second version of the *Madonna of the Rocks* painting, called *The Virgin of the Rocks*, can be found?

50. Which Eastern deity received gifts of frankincense and myrrh at his birth?

QUIZ 4

1. On what part of his body did Jacques Saunière have a birthmark?

2. At the start of *Deception Point*, who met Senator Sexton for breakfast at Toulos?

3. Who met at Castel Gandolfo with three of the most senior figures in the Vatican, to receive a large payment?

4. Robert Langdon tells Sophie that the Priory keystone is the map which reveals the hiding place of which of the following: the Priory of Sion Grand Master, the body of Jesus Christ, the Holy Grail or the bones of St Peter?

5. What item of stationery did Langdon use to push the wooden rose out of the lid of the box?

6. 'So dark the con of man' was an anagram of a painting by which artist?

7. What caused the door of the Zurich Depository Bank armoured car to explode outwards: a grenade, a bullet cartridge, a package containing semtex or an igniting hydrogen cylinder?

8. What was the name of the museum room in which Jacques Saunière grabbed and pulled down a Caravaggio painting?

9. In *Deception Point*, who overheard a secret meeting between Sexton and members of the Space Frontier Foundation, held in Sexton's apartment?

10. In *Angels and Demons*, the Large Hadron Collider is so large that it runs through the territory of two countries. What are they?

11. What item did Sophie find attached by a chain to the *Madonna of the Rocks* painting?

12. According to Langdon, which gender of bees outnumber the opposite gender by the Divine Proportion?

13. The head of the key found by Sophie was shaped as what symbol?

14. In *Deception Point*, when was the meteorite estimated to have landed on Earth: in the 15th Century, in the 17th Century or in the 18th Century?

15. The Atbash Cipher was based on which alphabet?

16. Who in *The Da Vinci Code* lodged in a place where locks were forbidden?

17. In *Angels and Demons*, the Hassassin knocked Vittoria out by bringing what part of his body down on her neck?

18. Which king did Pope Clement V work with to torture the Knights Templar: Phillipe IV, Louis III or Jean II?

19. In *Angels and Demons*, what was Leonardo Vetra's occupation?

20. The Knights Templar dwelled in the ruins of the Temple of Herod on the agreement of which king: King Baldwin II, King Louis I, King Richard I or King Galdofo II?

21. In which century was Temple Church founded: the 10th Century, the 12th Century, the 14th Century or the 16th Century?

22. Who was the Egyptian goddess of fertility?

23. In *Digital Fortress*, who had an invisible tap installed on Commander Strathmore's email and other communications systems?

24. How long was the Large Hadron Collider in *Angels and Demons*: 900 m, 2.7 km, 8 km or 27 km?

25. In *Angels and Demons*, which cardinal was strung from incensor cables in a church and burned to death: Cardinal Lamassé, Cardinal Ebner or Cardinal Guidera?

26. Where is the Vatican Observatory housed: at Castel Gandolfo, at St Peter's Basilica or at the Sistine Chapel?

27. According to *Digital Fortress*, in which US state is Fort Meade, the site of the NSA, situated?

28. Silas used to wear a strap to cause him pain, to remind him of Christ's suffering. What material was this strap made of?

29. In *Digital Fortress*, what were the last three words of the 'tattoo' written in magic marker on Megan's arm?

30. Which sport is Robert Langdon a keen player of: tennis, squash, water polo or chess?

31. What was the surname of the president of the Paris branch of the Depository Bank of Zurich?

32. In *Digital Fortress*, how old was Leland Fontaine?

33. Which cardinal in *Angels and Demons* was bound in heavy chains and drowned in the Fountain of the Four Rivers?

34. In *Deception Point*, who flew Sexton and Tolland to Tolland's ship: the Coast Guard, the US Navy or Special Ops forces?

35. In *Angels and Demons*, who was trapped under a casket and used a bone fragment to let in a little air?

36. In *Deception Point*, who was the section manager of the PODS team who admitted to Gabrielle Ashe that he had lied?

37. Which character in *The Da Vinci Code* flies out of Ciampino charter airport after a meeting near Rome?

38. In *Deception Point*, whose plan was to use a laser to heat the meteorite so that it would melt the ice above it and be easily extracted?

39. Which police officer in *The Da Vinci Code* wears a crux gemmata?

40. The air traffic controller at the English executive airport told Teabing there was a problem at the pumping station, as a reason for the change in the landing plans. What problem was this?

41. In *Angels and Demons*, how many storeys underground was Leonardo Vetra's private laboratory at CERN?

42. Which religious building in London has over 3,000 shrines or tombs?

43. In *Angels and Demons*, who shot and killed Captain Rocher: Lieutenant Chartrand, Robert Langdon or Commander Olivetti?

44. Who is the first person Silas contacts after murdering Saunière?

45. Which cardinal in *Angels and Demons* is first to be murdered: Cardinal Lamassé, Cardinal Baggia or Cardinal Ebner?

46. In *Digital Fortress*, who was killed with a non-invasive trauma bullet?

47. After Sophie and Langdon escape from Vernet, who is the first person Sophie shows the bank vault key to?

48. The dying Saunière laid himself out in a spreadeagled star shape in a homage to a famous sketch – by which Renaissance artist?

49. In *Angels and Demons*, was the church of Santa Maria della Vittoria the location of the murder of: the second cardinal, the third cardinal or the fourth cardinal?

50. Where did the first police shot to hit Silas strike him: his body, his arm or his leg?

QUIZ 5

1. According to the Priory, what was the name of the child born to Jesus and Mary Magdalene?

2. In *Digital Fortress*, who did Soshi Kuta alert that there was something strange occurring in the NSA's main databank?

3. When did Sir Leigh Teabing move to France to continue his search for the Holy Grail: five, 10, 15, 20 or 25 years ago?

4. According to *Angels and Demons*, four Illuminati scientists were branded in La Purga of 1668 – but with what symbol?

5. Who prevented Silas contacting his mentor by telephone?

6. In *Deception Point*, what was the first name of the marine geologist killed in the helicopter onboard the *Goya*?

7. In *Angels and Demons*, what was the name given to the cardinals who were favourites to be elected pope?

8. The word 'crucifix' came from the Latin verb 'cruciare'. What does this mean: to cleanse, to maim, to torture or to keep secret?

9. In *Digital Fortress*, Greg Hale is nicknamed after which mineral?

10. What did Sophie Neveu discover whilst searching for a birthday present from her grandfather: a map of the Rose Line, a mysterious key or a cryptex?

11. What was the title of the most senior handler of the Vatican's legal affairs?

12. We are told in *Angels and Demons* that the conclave to elect a new pope is held in which chapel?

13. What two words does Sophie understand the translation of 'Sang Real' to mean?

14. Which character with the initials RL was warned not to show his face by the Teacher?

15. In *Deception Point*, President Herney assembled his entire White House staff to hear the report on the meteorite from Rachel Sexton. How many of them were there: more than 80, more than 100, more than 120 or more than 140?

16. How many millions of dollars did Opus Dei's headquarters cost to build?

17. In *Angels and Demons*, who was taken captive by the Hassassin from Santa Maria della Vittoria church?

18. What was the name of the book about Sir Isaac Newton which led Sophie and Langdon to Westminster Abbey?

19. After Sophie's grandfather discovered Sophie rummaging through his private possessions, searching for her present for her ninth birthday, what chore did he set her?

20. When Langdon realises that he and Sophie need professional help to decode the mystery of the cryptex and the Holy Grail, who does he turn to?

21. What name was the Compass Rose originally known as?

22. The telephone despatcher at Snow Hill Division redirected Sophie's call to which policeman?

23. In *Angels and Demons*, what outdoor leisure pursuit did Langdon surprisingly see enacted indoors in a wind tunnel at CERN?

24. Sophie remembers seeing a woman involved in a sexual ritual with Jacques Saunière at his holiday home. What colour was her hair?

25. In *Angels and Demons*, who used a four-foot length of iron bar to attack the Hassassin?

26. On what day of the year was the birthday of the pre-Christian god, Mithras?

27. Can you name either of the people who dragged Silas out of Teabing's aircraft, out of sight of the English police?

28. In *Angels and Demons*, who found the antimatter trap deep within the catacombs: Camerlengo Ventresca, Vittoria Vetra, Maximilian Kohler or Robert Langdon?

29. Leigh Teabing says the Temple Church contains how many tombs?

30. Who designed the antimatter traps in *Angels and Demons*?

31. In *Digital Fortress*, at what university was David Becker a language professor?

32. According to Robert Langdon in *Angels and Demons*, what was the name of the first scientific think tank?

33. In *The Da Vinci Code*, how many sénéchaux are there?

34. When Sophie and Langdon are at the bank, how many door locks do they have to insert Saunière's key into before they come across a member of staff?

35. The *Mona Lisa* painting was produced using which style of painting: sfumato, Impressionism or Mannerist?

36. At what time of year did Sophie see her grandfather perform a sexual ritual: the spring equinox, midsummer, the autumn equinox or Christmas?

37. In *Angels and Demons*, who went through Leonardo Vetra's diaries and then flew to Rome?

38. In *Digital Fortress*, which NSA cryptographer was in communication with Tankado after Tankado had left the organisation?

39. What item did Bishop Aringarosa hand over to his pilot as payment?

40. Saunière wrote a message on the floor around his body using a watermark stylus. It was only visible under light of what colour?

41. According to Maximilian Kohler in *Angels and Demons*, the Big Bang theory was first proposed in 1927 by whom: Georges Lemaître, Edwin Hubble or Werner von Braun?

42. In *Deception Point*, how did Charles Brophy and his dog team die?

43. In *Angels and Demons*, who turned out to be the father of the camerlengo, Carlo Ventresca?

44. What was the name, beginning with the letter C, for the original icon depicting the female?

45. What was the first name of the official who lived in a luxury flat above the Depository Bank of Zurich?

46. In *Deception Point*, what NASA satellite system is based 120 miles up in space and measures ice forms?

47. In *Angels and Demons*, what was the name (in English or Italian) of the tunnel built between the Vatican and the Castle of the Angel?

48. How many letters does the password required to open the second cryptex contain?

49. In *Deception Point*, who urinates over themselves in order to prevent hammerhead sharks picking up the scent of their wound?

50. Bishop Aringarosa flew across the Atlantic to arrive at which European city?

1. What does 'Opus Dei' mean in English?

2. In *Digital Fortress*, who was the deputy director of the NSA?

3. In *Deception Point*, Delta-Two used a small, flying robot to help with surveillance of the NASA site in the Arctic. How long in centimetres was it?

4. Which French president commissioned the pyramid entrance to the Louvre museum?

5. Who caught the falling cryptex in Chapter House, only to crash to the ground and smash the vial holding the vinegar?

6. In *Deception Point*, who was the geologist who found the meteorite in the Arctic: Lawrence Ekstrom, Charles Brophy or Corky Marlinson?

7. What colour were the DCPJ officers' uniforms?

8. Who stopped the thief from stealing Aringarosa's offertory money in Spain?

9. In *Digital Fortress*, Midge states that someone installed a bypass switch to get past Gauntlet – who?

10. What colour was the silk interior of the wooden box containing Saunière's cryptex?

11. After Teabing is kidnapped by Rémy Legaludec, which London tube station do Langdon and Sophie enter?

12. On Bishop Aringarosa's second visit to Castel Gandolfo, what type of unmarked sedan car meets him: a Citroen, a Fiat, a Mercedes or an Alfa Romeo?

13. Silas was offered a room at the London Opus Dei centre on which floor?

14. Who threatened to destroy the *Madonna of the Rocks* painting to escape from the Louvre security warden?

15. In *Digital Fortress*, what was Strathmore's first name?

16. In *Deception Point*, who became trapped inside the Triton sub?

17. In *Digital Fortress*, what item of Megan's appeared to save Becker from a bullet fired by Hulohot?

18. How many letters are there in the Hebrew alphabet?

19. Which magazine had listed Langdon as one of its top ten most intriguing people?

20. In which Italian city do Robert Langdon and Sophie Neveu plan to meet a month or so after their visit to Rosslyn Chapel?

21. The wooded trail through Teabing's estate brings Langdon and the others out onto which highway?

22. Who suffered a wound to the stomach, which gave him 15 minutes to live?

23. In *Digital Fortress*, who used Susan Fletcher as a hostage to try to avoid being killed by Strathmore?

24. In *Angels and Demons*, who did Langdon and Vittoria spot following them in St Peter's Square: Lieutenant Chartrand, Chinita Macri, Cardinal Mortati or Gunter Glick?

25. According to *Deception Point*, from what distance can a hammerhead shark smell blood: up to half a mile away, three quarters of a mile away or a mile away?

26. Which Parisian building holds 65,300 pieces of art, according to Robert Langdon?

27. Which violin-maker used the Divine Proportion in calculations to do with his craft?

28. Who helped, along with Langdon, to explain the true meaning of the Grail to Sophie?

29. In *Deception Point*, what five-letter acronym is used to describe the US President?

30. What symbol has been worn into the floor of Rosslyn Chapel by the feet of thousands of visitors?

31. What flower-based name is given to the north-to-south longitude line?

32. Where did Silas hide his cellphone in his room?

33. Which church in England is completely round in shape and is visited by Langdon and the others?

34. Who was the only person who knew the Teacher's real identity and was killed for this knowledge?

35. The women in Saunière's grotto who performed an ancient ritual wore shoes of what colour: white, silver or golden?

36. Which Illuminati sculptor are we told in *Angels and Demons* created *The Ecstacy of St Teresa*?

37. Who carries a driver's pistol on leaving the Depository Bank of Zurich?

38. Can you name three of the seven words suggested unsuccessfully on Teabing's aircraft to open the second cryptex?

39. What colour was the robe of Jesus in the painting, *The Last Supper*?

40. What served as a bed in Silas's room in Paris?

41. Which artist's name was an anagram of the phrase, 'O Draconian devil!'?

42. Which relative of the Rosslyn Chapel verger is the head of the Rosslyn Trust?

43. How much had the winning bid been for Da Vinci's Codex Leicester, to the nearest million dollars?

44. In the Fibonaci sequence left behind by Jacques Saunière, what number followed 5 and 8?

45. What was the keyword which opened the second cryptex?

46. Teabing states that the word 'rose' is identical in which three languages?

47. Which one of the following was not under surveillance from the advanced centre found on Teabing's estate: Jacques Saunière, Colbert Sostaque, André Vernet or Edouard Desrochers?

48. In two Dan Brown books, Robert Langdon carries an item in his jacket which is used by two European women. What sort of item is it?

49. Who was killed first: Rémy, the sénéchaux or Saunière?

50. When Teabing's car reaches the city, which London church does it head for?

1. Under Christianity, which pagan god's trident became the devil's pitchfork?

2. In *Deception Point*, who died on the *Goya* as the megaplume and giant whirlpool sucked the ship down?

3. Can you name two of the four Tarot card suits?

4. What is the name of the private viewing area in the Louvre in which the *Mona Lisa* was located?

5. In *Digital Fortress*, what was the full name of the email organization known by the letters ARA?

6. To which hospital was Bishop Aringarosa taken after being shot?

7. What was the name of the castle in *Angels and Demons* in which the Hassassin held Vittoria captive?

8. At the end of *Digital Fortress*, the ring that David Becker gave Susan Fletcher was made from what metal?

9. In *Deception Point*, there is a security test to enter the NRO building in which a human substance is checked for the correct DNA. Which human substance is this?

10. Moments before someone dies in *Angels and Demons*, they give Robert Langdon a Sony Ruvi camcorder. Who is this?

11. Who planned to install a back door in *Digital Fortress* to make it breakable by the NSA?

12. In *Angels and Demons*, what was the Pope believed to have died from: pneumonia, a stroke, a heart attack or cancer?

13. What were discovered at Nag Hammadi in 1945: the Coptic Scrolls, the Dead Sea Scrolls, or the Hammadian Scrolls?

14. What was the name of the French tennis stadium close to which Langdon and Sophie travelled?

15. What type of paper was the verse inside the first cryptex written on: parchment, papyrus or vellum?

16. What type of aircraft was Teabing's personal plane: a Hawker 731, a Lear Jet, a Britten-Norman Islander or a Beechcraft Baron?

17. Which French police officer organised the tape recording of Fache and Langdon's conversation in the Louvre's Grand Gallery?

18. What alcoholic drink did Rémy Legaludec take from the limousine bar, whilst the others were inside Temple Church?

19. In *Angels and Demons*, what is the name of the force responsible for security at the Vatican City?

20. How many disciples are portrayed in the painting, *The Last Supper*?

21. In *Digital Fortress*, what turned out to be the numeric kill code to stop the worm from opening up the NSA databank to outsiders?

22. When the forensics torch was shone onto the covering of the *Mona Lisa*, what colour did the words glow?

23. In *Digital Fortress*, what are we told is the name of the oldest section of Seville, which has no roads but only narrow walkways?

24. According to Robert Langdon in *Angels and Demons*, from which religion did the Nazis take the swastika symbol?

25. Who took Silas in, shortly after his escape from prison?

26. The US Embassy in Paris is located on which avenue: Avenue des Salles, Avenue Gabriel or Avenue Principe?

27. Which police officer met Langdon at his hotel in Paris the night of Saunière's murder?

28. In *Angels and Demons*, who believes that an attempt on their life occurs while they are studying in the Vatican Archives?

29. What is the name of Langdon's editor in New York: Edward Nkune, Jonas Faukman, Bill Wainright or Richard Jackson?

30. In *Digital Fortress*, who installed a keypress recording chip into Susan Fletcher's keyboard inside Node 3?

31. In *Angels and Demons*, Langdon demonstrates to Vittoria that a piece of US currency is covered in Illuminati symbology, including a pyramid. Which piece of currency is this?

32. In *Deception Point*, what was Delta Force's PH2: a stun gun, a micro robot, an attack helicopter or their encoded portable communications device?

33. Can you name two of the three words the King's College librarian first types into the computer database to assist Langdon and Sophie with their search for the correct tomb?

34. Who, whilst escaping the French police, makes a reverse-charge call to New York?

35. In *Deception Point*, what becomes the new name of SETI – the Search for Extraterrestrial Intelligence?

36. In the painting, *The Last Supper*, what is the colour of the hair of the disciple who sits on the right of Jesus?

37. Shrimpus Uglius From Hellus is a creature which appears in a computer database in which of Dan Brown's books?

38. In *Digital Fortress*, Commander Strathmore's final word before he died was a name. Whose?

39. Bishop Aringarosa suffered a broken nose when he was a young missionary – in which European country?

40. At the end of *The Da Vinci Code*, where does Robert Langdon conclude that the Grail may lie?

41. What 164-foot tall structure stands in Paris as a monument to Napoleon?

42. In *Digital Fortress*, who is the first to believe that Hale is North Dakota?

43. At which hour of the night does Silas visit the Church of Saint-Sulpice: 9 pm, 11 pm, 1 am or 3 am?

44. In whose office in the Louvre do the French police set up their command centre?

45. In *Angels and Demons*, a bullet from Robert Langdon's gun hits which part of the Hassassin's body?

46. In the four-line verse which accompanies the second cryptex, which city is mentioned?

47. Which of Paris's art museums, viewable from the Tuileries Gardens, is a converted railway station?

48. Who made a phone call to the US Embassy, pretending to be Robert Langdon?

49. According to *Digital Fortress*, what university hosted the very first computer, the Mark 1?

50. Which of the following is a descendent of the first Duke of Lancaster: David Becker, Leigh Teabing or Marie Chauvel?

QUIZ 8

1. Whose favourite Da Vinci work turned out to be the *Vitruvian Man* sketch?

2. In which Asian city does the Depository Bank of Zurich have a branch: Manilla, Bangkok, Seoul or Kuala Lumpur?

3. After Rémy releases the monk outside Temple Church, who does he first hold at gunpoint?

4. Who surprisingly handed back the second cryptex to Robert Langdon, whilst holding him at gunpoint?

5. In *Angels and Demons*, Camerlengo Ventresca carries the antimatter, just minutes before it is due to detonate, into what vehicle?

6. According to Langdon's recollections, which Mason is the most senior: a 27-degree Mason, a 30-degree Mason or a 32-degree Mason?

7. In *Digital Fortress*, on what day of the week does David Becker arrive in Spain?

8. The first person Langdon and Sophie encounter inside the Depository Bank of Zurich greets them in which two languages?

9. In *Digital Fortress*, who pulls a gun on Susan Fletcher and refuses to give her the password to his personal elevator?

10. In *Angels and Demons*, who uses white cotton gloves and finger cymbals to study Galileo's manuscript in the Vatican Archives?

11. After Langdon hears Sophie's phone-message instructions, he heads into which room in the Louvre museum?

12. In *Digital Fortress*, what is the name of the director of the NSA?

13. In *Deception Point*, who is manoeuvred by Marjorie Tench in a CNN debate to state that they might abolish NASA if elected to be president?

14. What is the name of the princess in Walt Disney's *Sleeping Beauty* who is codenamed 'Rose'?

15. Langdon says that the male symbol derives from which god, named after a planet?

16. In *Deception Point*, who rides in the helicopter that attacks the *Goya*, apart from the three Delta Force agents?

17. According to *Angels and Demons*, the Vatican's 1,407 rooms house how many works of art: over 20,000, over 40,000 or over 60,000?

18. What name, beginning with the letter G, was given to the sundial-like device found in the floor of Saint-Sulpice?

19. What was the name of the female glaciologist in *Deception Point*?

20. In *Digital Fortress*, what job does Midge Milken have at the NSA: internal security analyst, systems operator or head of governmental affairs?

21. In *Deception Point*, how many pairs of legs does the fossil found inside the meteorite have?

22. What sort of business is found at Number 24 Rue Haxo?

23. The stretch limousine which awaits Teabing at Biggin Hill airport is what make of car?

24. Who is descended from the Jewish House of Benjamin: St Peter, Mary Magdalene or Jesus Christ?

25. Before the establishment of the Greenwich meridian, zero degrees longitude ran through which city?

26. Hieros Gamos is a spiritual ceremony. Langdon tells Sophie that the name comes from which language?

27. In *The Da Vinci Code*, Langdon was originally leaving Paris on what day of the week?

28. When Silas smashes the floor tiles, what item of clothing does he use to dull the sound?

29. Teabing says that the Dead Sea Scrolls were discovered in which decade of the 20th Century?

30. Whose Interpol crime report included petty theft and not paying for an emergency tracheotomy operation?

31. In *Deception Point*, Ashe goes to a friend at the ABC news network for advice. What is this friend's name?

32. In *Digital Fortress*, what make of sedan car does Susan Fletcher drive?

33. When Bishop Aringarosa is in hospital, who does he ask Captain Fache to give the 20 million euros to?

34. The night wardens of the Louvre were taken into which wing for questioning?

35. 'The End of Days' is a name given to the period when a certain astrological age ends and another begins – but by which institution?

36. From the Tuileries Gardens, what can be seen to the west: the Pompidou Centre, the Louvre or the Musée du Jeu de Paume?

37. In *Deception Point*, what substance is pumped into a NASA Mark IX microclimate suit to help regulate the temperature in hot and cold climes?

38. Who had shared the secrets of the *Mona Lisa* in an outreach scheme nicknamed 'Culture for Convicts'?

39. What is the name of a book written in the 1930s by Opus Dei's founder, which has been translated into 42 languages? The title is made up of two words, of three letters each.

40. In *Digital Fortress*, who is eating his third calzone pizza when Midge Milken first calls him about Strathmore and TRANSLTR?

41. Which Parisian museum curator received a copy of Langdon's latest manuscript?

42. In *Digital Fortress*, what was the name of the unbreakable code algorithm which used rotating cleartext?

43. Who was Grand Master of the Priory of Sion between the years 1510 and 1519?

44. Rosslyn Chapel stands seven miles south of which city?

45. In which Dan Brown novel did Langdon first visit the Vatican?

46. In Saint-Sulpice, what structure interrupts the route of the Rose Line across the floor of the church?

47. Which side of the *Mona Lisa* looks bigger due to a painting trick of lowering the background?

48. In *Deception Point*, Rachel Sexton is whisked from the Eastern Seaboard of the United States deep into the Arctic Circle in what sort of fighter jet?

49. At Temple Church, who plays the part of Mr Christopher Wren the Fourth?

50. How many rooms did the dwelling on the second floor of the Church of Saint-Sulpice have?

QUIZ 9

1. Which church figure was Silas's mentor?

2. Langdon says that the son of Isis provided inspiration for images of the Virgin Mary nursing the infant Jesus. What was his name?

3. In *Angels and Demons*, CERN employs how many of the world's particle physicists: one quarter, over half or over two thirds of all the world's particle physicists?

4. Each of the discs of Saunière's first cryptex had how many letters written around the rim?

5. Was the name of the Executive Services Officer at Biggin Hill: James Brekard, Richard Woodhouse or Simon Edwards?

6. By what name was the Priory of Sion's military wing best-known?

7. In *Angels and Demons*, when Vittoria and Langdon first spot the camera which is broadcasting images of the antimatter trap in the Vatican, how many hours are left on the countdown clock?

8. The document covering the second cryptex had four lines of verse written on it. What was the last word of those four lines?

9. How many floors of Opus Dei's headquarters contained chapels?

10. Allegedly, the Knights Templar found the Holy Grail documents under which temple?

11. Was Robert Langdon: married, single, engaged to be married or a widower?

12. What was the first word Sophie used in an attempt to open her grandfather's cryptex?

13. The French policeman, Collet, has what rank?

14. After the deception in Saint-Sulpice, whom did Silas call: Bishop Aringarosa, Robert Langdon, the Teacher or Marie Chauvel?

15. In *Digital Fortress*, David Becker chases and jumps onto a bus. What number is the bus: 27, 38, 116 or 203?

16. In *Deception Point*, according to Senator Sedgewick Sexton, for how many years has NASA been engaged in a search for extra-terrestrial life?

17. In *Angels and Demons*, what number vault in the Vatican Archive was the repository for manuscripts and works by Galileo?

18. Who lends Robert Langdon their cellphone, so he can make a call to what he thinks is the US Embassy?

19. In *Deception Point*, what was the name of the old NASA launch site where Rachel Sexton arrives to meet the US President?

20. The LCD screen at the Depository Bank of Zurich displayed instructions in how many languages: three, five or seven?

21. Saint-Sulpice was built over the ruins of a temple dedicated to which goddess?

22. What artwork was an anagram of the phrase, 'Oh, lame saint!'?

23. Who did Silas kill at Saint-Sulpice, shortly after discovering he had been tricked by Saunière and the three sénéchaux?

24. In *Digital Fortress*, who killed Greg Hale?

25. Who manages to carry a gun through the metal detector gate at Westminster Abbey?

26. In *Digital Fortress*, who was sprayed in the face with a pepper spray at Seville airport?

27. In *Deception Point*, what type of creature was the fossil inside the meteorite: an isopod, a marine mollusc or a dragonfly?

28. What did Teabing find distasteful, apart from French politics and taxes?

29. In *Angels and Demons*, which cardinal announced that he had been Devil's Advocate when the previous Pope had been elected?

30. In *Digital Fortress*, what was the name, beginning with the letter B, of the Cause and Effect Simulator used by the NSA to map out scenarios?

31. In *Deception Point*, what was the name of Michael Tolland's weekly TV series?

32. In *Digital Fortress*, what was the name of the punk who killed himself a year before Becker arrived in Seville?

33. Robert Langdon usually managed how many laps of the university swimming pool: five, 15 or 50?

34. In *The Da Vinci Code*, which Parisian police officer is referred to as 'le Taureau' – the bull?

35. From the Tuileries Gardens, which famed art museum can you see to the south?

36. In *Deception Point*, what is the name of the Chairman of Paleontology at UCLA who meets an icy end?

37. What was the last word scrawled by Jacques Saunière on the glass covering of the *Mona Lisa*?

38. Whose name do the French judicial police discover in Saunière's daily planner?

39. In *Deception Point*, Rachel Sexton worked for which American organisation?

40. Who was the author of *The Lost Language of Ideograms*: Sir Leigh Teabing, Robert Langdon or Jacques Saunière?

41. What five-letter word opened Saunière's first cryptex?

42. In *Deception Point*, what is the figure (given in billions of US dollars) for NASA's budget?

43. According to *Angels and Demons*, what was the secret Illuminati number: 666, 109, 503 or 97?

44. How many pounds does Teabing offer his pilot to fly Langdon, Sophie and Silas as well as himself and Rémy?

45. What appropriate type of wood was the box that carried Saunière's cryptex?

46. When Saunière's passcode number was arranged in the Fibonacci number sequence, what single number comprised both the first and last digit?

47. What brand of expensive watch on Vernet's arm nearly gives him away when escaping with Langdon and Neveu?

48. The Priory of Sion was founded in 1099 in which city?

49. In *Angels and Demons*, who was the author of the book, *God, Miracles and the New Physics*: Leonardo Vetra, Maximilian Kohler or Cardinal Mortati?

50. What was the name given to the code-writing scheme produced by Ancient Roman leader, Julius Caesar?

QUIZ 10

1. What was the name of the cross which bore 13 jewels: crux templar, crux gemmata, crux diamante or crux sion?

2. When was the last time the *Mona Lisa* painting was stolen: 1872, 1911, 1943 or 1968?

3. Who was the author of *The Symbology of Secret Sects*?

4. Who was in the Louvre's men's toilet when Langdon entered?

5. What is the name of the murdered German cardinal in *Angels and Demons*?

6. On what material was a secret held inside a cryptex traditionally written?

7. Who is the owner of the Numatech Corporation in *Digital Fortress*?

8. Who painted *The Last Supper*, which is found in the Santa Maria delle Grazie?

9. In *Digital Fortress*, what part of the NSA is located 214 feet below ground, created by the removal of 250 million metric tons of earth?

10. Which character in *The Da Vinci Code* fell down a well shaft as a child and almost perished?

11. What flower is the Priory of Sion's official symbol, according to Robert Langdon?

12. In *Deception Point*, what was the nationality of the beer the NASA administrator has flown in from Greenland to toast their discovery?

13. Which French police officer wielded a Manurhin MR-93 revolver?

14. In *Deception Point*, who was knocked out by ice bullets fired by Delta Force?

15. Robert Langdon tells Sophie that the halos of Catholic saints were derived from sun disks from where: Babylonia, Egypt, Greece or India?

16. The Opus Dei centre in London overlooks which gardens?

17. In *Deception Point*, Xavia and Corky measured the meteorite sample for what: titanium content, molybendium content or zirconium content?

18. Saunière's first cryptex was constructed of what sort of stone?

19. How many thousands of tombs does the King's College librarian tell Langdon can be found in London?

20. What was the official religion of Ancient Rome at the time that the first Bible was put together?

21. Which Scottish building had Sophie visited before as a young child?

22. In *The Da Vinci Code*, what does 'PTS' stand for?

23. In *Angels and Demons*, who holds Vittoria and Langdon captive at first in his office in Vatican City before coming to believe their story?

24. Jacques Saunière's holiday home was located in which region of France?

25. What nationality was Sir Leigh Teabing's manservant?

26. Which knight was buried in Westminster Abbey in the presence of his friend, Alexander Pope?

27. What field of policework is Sophie Neveu engaged in?

28. In the Louvre, were any of the security cameras fakes?

29. In *Digital Fortress*, what part of Cloucharde's body was fitted with a plaster cast: his left ankle, his right wrist, his left arm or his right leg?

30. What was the name of the pope who issued a papal bull making the Knights Templar a law unto themselves: Pious IX, Clement V or Innocent II?

31. In *Deception Point*, who had worked for many years in the Pentagon: Lawrence Ekstrom, Michael Tolland or Zach Herney?

32. What name is given to the long central section of a church?

33. Which creature inspired inspire Vittoria Vetra's antimatter trap design in *Angels and Demons*: hermit crabs, Portuguese man-o'-wars or trapdoor spiders?

34. Who taught Sophie the language found on the wooden rose?

35. What does 'Portatore' mean on Vatican bearer bonds: only cardinals can cash them in, they are fake or anyone holding them can cash them in?

36. In *Deception Point*, how many satellites made up NASA's EOS project: five, seven, nine or 17?

37. What was Robert Langdon's nickname on campus?

38. In *Angels and Demons*, at which door did Langdon, Vetra and Kohler discover the eyeball: at the door to St Peter's Basilica, at the door to the Large Hadron Collider or at the door to CERN's Haz-Mat Chamber?

39. What name did Langdon give to the shortened trip around the Louvre taken by most tourists?

40. Which London University college had an extensive theological computer database?

41. In *Angels and Demons*, what was the name of the second-in-command in the Swiss Guard?

42. Who positioned Jacques Saunière's body so oddly at the murder scene?

43. The HSCT craft which carried Langdon in *Angels and Demons* was capable of flying at what speed: Mach 6, Mach 9 or Mach 15?

44. What is the lily flower called in French?

45. In *Deception Point*, which one of the following is not given as a nickname for the White House's Oval Office: The Lobster Trap, Ronnie's Rumpus Room, Dick's Den or the Loo?

46. What was the name of the doctor who treated Robert Langdon after his exploits in *Angels and Demons*: Dr Henrik, Dr Rancontelli, Dr Jacobus or Dr Nkune?

47. According to the Priory of Sion, what sex was the child born to Jesus and Mary Magdalene?

48. What was the first drink Sophie had after escaping with Langdon from the Louvre?

49. Which of the four cardinals in *Angels and Demons* was branded with the Illuminati sign, 'water'?

50. When Silas broke the neck of a dockworker, he was stealing a case of what foodstuff?

QUIZ 11

1. In *The Da Vinci Code*, what is stated to be the longest building in Europe?

2. In which month of the year did Langdon, Sophie and Teabing all descend upon Westminster Abbey?

3. How many entrances and exits were there to the Salle des Etats in the Louvre?

4. From which god, named after a planet, does Langdon say the female symbol derives?

5. In *Deception Point*, which chain-smoking member of the President's team seeks to trick Senator Sexton on a CNN debate show?

6. Which one of the following is not a card in a Tarot deck: the Great Redeemer, the Female Pope or the Empress?

7. What did Sophie, Teabing and Langdon use to bind Silas?

8. On which floor of the new Opus Dei headquarters can you find a chapel: the sixth floor, the eighth floor or the thirteenth floor?

9. How old had Sophie been when her parents died in a car crash?

10. Can you name two of the four major rivers commemorated in Bernini's Fountain of the Four Rivers in *Angels and Demons*?

11. Was Sophie Neveu: divorced, engaged or never married?

12. How much did TRANSLTR cost to construct in *Digital Fortress*, to the nearest hundred million dollars?

13. What sort of vehicle in *Deception Point* was under control of Commander Wayne Loosigian: a space shuttle, a fighter jet, an attack helicopter or a nuclear submarine?

14. What word was branded on the first cardinal to be murdered in *Angels and Demons*?

15. What three-digit code did Sophie Neveu give Langdon to access a phone-message box?

16. What was the only four-letter word scrawled on the glass covering of the *Mona Lisa* by Jacques Saunière?

17. In the 5th Century, Jesus Christ's bloodline allegedly mixed with the bloodline of royalty from which country?

18. Who was entrusted with the task of opening the first cryptex?

19. In *Angels and Demons*, how many Illuminati brands did there turn out to be?

20. In *Deception Point*, which US organisation was based at Fairfax, Virginia?

21. Can you name either of the two bright colours found on the Swiss Guards' tunics in *Angels and Demons*?

22. In *Digital Fortress*, what make of gun did Strathmore wield during the standoff with Hale?

23. Which Louvre gallery housed the museum's most famous examples of Italian art?

24. In the painting, *The Last Supper*, what colour is Jesus's cloak?

25. In *Deception Point*, Senator Sexton has a fateful press conference designed to uncover the evidence of the fake meteorite at the base of which giant obelisk?

26. Vernet drove Langdon and Sophie out of the bank in what number armoured car?

27. According to *Angels and Demons*, the Swiss Guard get around Rome in what brand of car?

28. The address written on the back of Saunière's key was close to a stadium which hosted which sport?

29. How old was Jacques Saunière when he died: 69, 73 or 76?

30. In *Digital Fortress*, how many US dollars did the fat German tourist claim to have spent on hiring his red-haired escort for the weekend?

31. How many cards are there in a Tarot card pack?

32. Who is a Professor of Religious Symbology?

33. Who gives Fache a tip-off that Langdon and Sophie had not travelled by train: Opus Dei, Interpol, the CIA or Scotland Yard?

34. Sigisbert was the son of which French king: Thalbert, Clement, Claubert or Dagobert?

35. According to Sophie Neveu, how many possible permutations are there for a ten-digit password and account number: 55 million, 100 million, 10 billion or 100 billion?

36. Measuring one's hip to the floor and dividing it by the measurement of one's knee to the floor yields a figure close to which of the following: 0.696, 1.302, 1.618 or 1.999?

37. Which reporter in *Angels and Demons* has a red beard?

38. According to Teabing, after the crucifixion of Jesus Christ, Mary Magdalene fled to which country?

39. How many phone numbers were inside the sealed envelope opened by Sister Sandrine?

40. Can you name all four of the elemental Illuminati brands in *Angels and Demons*?

41. Who follows the Rose Line through Paris several days after the main events in *The Da Vinci Code*?

42. Who called Interpol regarding Langdon and Sophie Neveu's escape: Collet, Teabing or Fache?

43. Who had managed to meet with Jacques Saunière by pretending they had information about the deaths of some of his family members?

44. From the Tuileries Gardens, which famed art museum can you see to the east?

45. In *Deception Point*, which Delta Force team member was the first to perish?

46. Who was the first monarch to be crowned in Westminster Abbey?

47. In *Angels and Demons*, Cardinal Lamassé was found with his lungs punctured, dressed up as what sort of figure?

48. Which organisation transferred almost one billion dollars into the Vatican Bank in 1982?

49. Who offered his pilot a 10,000 euro bond to change their plane's flight route?

50. In *Digital Fortress*, who appeared to call security but only faked the call during the standoff with Greg Hale?

QUIZ 12

1. During Sophie's discussions about the Holy Grail with Langdon and Teabing, which Biblical figure does she label a prostitute?

2. In *Angels and Demons*, at what time was the antimatter expected to explode, causing massive devastation?

3. The disembodied hand in the painting, *The Last Supper*, holds what item?

4. What was the name of the bank in which Langdon and Sophie discovered Saunière's cryptex held in a deposit box?

5. Who in *Deception Point* suffered White Death?

6. What colour are the robes worn by Westminster Abbey's volunteer guides?

7. The official Priory symbol for the Grail is a rose with how many petals?

8. What object does Neveu press the GPS tracking dot into before throwing it?

9. Which one of the scientists in *Deception Point* was the winner of a National Medal of Science for work in astrophysics?

10. What is the name of the London garden which holds the oldest living fruit trees in Great Britain?

11. At the start of *The Da Vinci Code*, in which hotel is Robert Langdon staying?

12. Which flower is sometimes used to mark north on a compass rose instead of an arrowhead?

13. In *Digital Fortress*, the words on Tankado's ring were written in which ancient language?

14. Saunière's cryptex was comprised of how many marble discs?

15. What was the name of the Egyptian god that an Essex County prisoner stated was also a brand of condoms?

16. Who mentions the 1950 renovations, when stating that Teabing is wrong about the 10 tombs in Temple Church: Reverend Knowles, Robert Langdon or the altar boy?

17. At the deposit bank, how many attempts do you get to enter the correct account number in the terminal before it locks itself?

18. Can you name three of the six car makes in Teabing's collection in France?

19. Once Silas is inside Temple Church, who does he grab?

20. What was 'The Witches' Hammer' used by the Church: a sacred symbol, a book or a torture tool?

21. To ancient peoples, what did the pentacle represent: the masculine side of the world, the daytime, the feminine side or the night time?

22. Scholars investigating the Mystery of Sheshach used the Atbash Cipher to reveal which Biblical city?

23. In *Angels and Demons*, what was the name of the BBC camerawoman who worked with Gunter Glick?

24. Who left Paris in the cargo-hold of an armoured car?

25. Before Langdon explained the true meaning of the Holy Grail to Sophie Neveu, what did she think it was?

26. In *Digital Fortress*, whose charred body did Strathmore have to move before he could reset the power for TRANSLTR?

27. In *Deception Point*, in which aircraft did Rachel Sexton first meet the President of the United States?

28. What colour SmartCar did Sophie Neveu drive?

29. The viewing capsules of which London attraction reminded Langdon of sarcophagi?

30. What was the name of the astronomer at the Vatican Observatory who had met Bishop Aringarosa on his previous visit: Father Santori, Father Mangano or Father Baggia?

31. What is the nickname of Château Villette:
    Le Petite Anglais, La Castille de Revolution
    or La Petite Versailles?

32. Which character in *The Da Vinci Code* has a
    lethal peanut allergy?

33. At the end of *Digital Fortress*, who is flown
    back in a Lear 60 from Spain to the United
    States?

34. Sophie is shocked to find that one of the
    figures in *The Last Supper* looks like a woman.
    Is this the figure to the immediate right of
    Jesus, the immediate left of Jesus, the far right
    or the far left?

35. Who, standing in Teabing's kitchen, sees a
    TV news broadcast identifying Langdon and
    Sophie Neveu?

36. What household item was required to read the
    crimson ink writing of Da Vinci's Codex
    Leicester?

37. In *Angels and Demons*, what is the name of
    the MSNBC reporter who breaks the news of
    the first two murdered cardinals?

38. What was the name of the Italian airport at which Bishop Aringarosa arrives after his transatlantic flight?

39. Langdon and the others flee from Teabing's château in what vehicle?

40. In *Angels and Demons*, who grabs the videotape of Cardinal Lamassé's murder from Chinita Macri's belt?

41. What flower did the Ancient Romans used to hang above meetings to show that the meeting was secret?

42. Which character in *The Da Vinci Code* was a former British Royal Historian?

43. What room at the Château Villette had Teabing converted into his giant study?

44. What flower formed part of the inlay in the lid of the box that held Saunière's cryptex?

45. In *Deception Point*, who first suggests to Gabrielle Ashe that Senator Sexton is taking large and illegal campaign contributions from private space and aerospace companies?

46. In *Digital Fortress*, how many fingers does Ensei Tankado have on each hand?

47. What is the name of the librarian at King's College who assists Langdon and Neveu?

48. In *Angels and Demons*, what part of Leonardo Vetra's body does the Hassassin cut out to break through a security system in CERN?

49. What make of car had the Teacher arranged for Silas to drive whilst in Paris?

50. How many Grand Masters of the Priory of Sion were English or Irish and with the first name, Robert?

QUIZ 13

1. Bishop Aringarosa picks up a cellphone message in Italy which he thinks is from the Teacher but turns out to be from what other character?

2. In *Digital Fortress*, who was engulfed in the inferno caused by TRANSLTR's burning processors?

3. Who had phoned Sophie Neveu the afternoon of his murder, telling her that she may be in grave danger?

4. What is the name of the executive airfield where Teabing's aircraft is housed: Le Bourget, Ciampino or Louviers?

5. In *The Da Vinci Code*, who fears he has missed calls from the Teacher due to poor cellphone reception in the mountains?

6. In *Deception Point*, who is described as a cross between Carl Sagan and Jacques Cousteau?

7. In *Angels and Demons*, we are told that Robert Langdon drives what type of sports car: a Saab 900, a BMW 5 series or a Mercedes?

8. What were those searching for the Grail looking for in Westminster Abbey to break the code: a cross, an orb or a letter M?

9. According to Langdon, when was the last rumoured sighting of the Holy Grail: 1347, 1447, 1547 or 1647?

10. Did Sir Leigh Teabing: wear leg braces, walk with crutches or require both leg braces and crutches?

11. In *Deception Point*, how many members were there in the Delta Force team sent to eliminate Rachel Sexton and the civilian scientists?

12. Which British knight and scientist had once been a Grand Master of the Priory of Sion?

13. In *Deception Point*, how many white envelopes did Senator Sexton prepare, containing proof that the meteorite was a fraud?

14. In *Digital Fortress*, what happened to the worm after the NSA entered their first attempt at the kill code?

15. Which novel by Victor Hugo does Langdon tell Sophie is a Grail allegory?

16. Sophie estimates that her grandfather's cryptex contains how many millions of different permutations for the password?

17. How many Knights Templar originally excavated the ruined Temple of Herod: six, nine, 12 or 14?

18. Which character in *Angels and Demons* organised the deaths of four cardinals and a pope and then kills himself by covering his body in oils and igniting them?

19. In what year did Father Josemaría Escrivá die: 1975, 1982, 1994 or 2000?

20. In *Angels and Demons*, which famous artist and sculptor are we told designed the Swiss Guard uniforms: Da Vinci, Michelangelo or Bernini?

21. In *Angels and Demons*, which river does the Church of Illumination overlook?

22. After Collet had been at the Depository Bank of Zurich, to which château did he head with five other police cars?

23. In *Digital Fortress*, what item did Strathmore throw onto the landing to convince Hale he was upstairs rather than downstairs?

24. In *Deception Point*, what was the name given to the room onboard the *Charlotte* from which virtually no sound could escape?

25. Can you recall the number that comprises the Divine Proportion, to the nearest tenth?

26. In *Deception Point*, can you name two of the five space companies that met with Sexton at his private apartment?

27. Who launched a metal rubbish can through a Louvre window to send the police off on the wrong track?

28. Who cut Silas free of his bonds whilst in the limousine parked in London?

29. In *Digital Fortress*, who sent David Becker to Spain on a mission to obtain Tankado's possessions?

30. In *Deception Point*, the micro robot piloted by Delta Force crashes into which part of Wailee Ming's body, causing him to fall into the extraction hole and die?

31. Rosslyn Chapel had been modelled by the Knights Templar on the design of what building in Jerusalem?

32. In *Deception Point*, which former American president was President Zachary Herney's idol?

33. Which figure in the painting, *The Last Supper*, is making a threatening, slicing gesture across their throat?

34. At the rectory house in Rosslyn Chapel, Sophie Neveu is reunited with which two of her relatives?

35. According to *Deception Point*, which one of the
     following had not seen a ghost in the Lincoln
     Bedroom: Winston Churchill, Nancy Reagan or
     Amy Carter?

36. In which English county did Teabing's plane
     land?

37. How tall was the Louvre's La Pyramide: 55 feet,
     71 feet, 89 feet or 108 feet?

38. What was the name of the famous sketch by
     Da Vinci which Robert Langdon recalled, after
     viewing the dead curator in the Louvre?

39. What was the first food Sophie had after
     escaping from the Louvre with Langdon?

40. Who helped Langdon and Neveu, only to
     turn on them with a gun after hearing of the
     murders of the three sénéchaux?

41. How big was Saunière's cryptex: about the size
     of a tennis ball can, a toilet roll, a rifle barrel,
     or a food tin?

42. Who, in *Deception Point*, hands Gabrielle Ashe
     a red folder containing explicit photos of
     Ashe's affair?

43. At which museum does Robert Langdon first meet Sophie Neveu?

44. According to Teabing, how many different gospels were originally considered to be included in the New Testament of the Bible: more than 20, more than 40, more than 60 or more than 80?

45. How old is Rachel Sexton in *Deception Point*: 29, 34 or 37?

46. According to Teabing, which Roman emperor helped put together the first Bible?

47. Whose desk features a two-foot tall model of an ancient knight?

48. In *Deception Point*, who does the Delta Force team kill first?

49. In *Angels and Demons*, Vittoria Vetra discovered that the unknown Illuminati sculptor is whom: Michelangelo, Gianlorenzo Bernini or Raphael Santi?

50. By the time Langdon and Sophie reach King's College, London, in whose possession is the first cryptex?

1. In which item in Saunière's office have bugging devices been hidden?

2. In *Deception Point*, what feature, beginning with the letter, C, does Corky Marlinson maintain is only found in meteorites and not on Earth?

3. Who was Godefroi de Bouillon: the head of the Knights Templar, the pope who ordered the purge of the Priory and Knights Templar or the founder of the Priory of Sion?

4. In *Angels and Demons*, which murdered cardinal was found at the base of an obelisk in St Peter's Square: the first, the second or the third?

5. In *Deception Point*, which member of the Delta Force team did Tolland capture using the robot arms of his submersible?

6. What is the first of the Gnostic Gospels Teabing quotes from: the Gospel of Philip, the Gospel of Mary Magdalene or the Gospel of Saul?

7. Silas believed the keystone was located in which French church: Saint-Sulpice, Saint Francis or Saint Gabriel?

8. What three letters are also known as the Divine Proportion?

9. In *Deception Point*, Rachel Sexton sends a fax proving the meteorite to be a fraud – but to whose office?

10. Which French artist and film maker was the Priory's Grand Master before Jacques Saunière?

11. What part of Vernet's body suffered severe injury shortly after he held Langdon and Neveu at gunpoint?

12. What denomination of British banknotes did Teabing remove from his aircraft wall-safe to act as documentation for Sophie and Langdon?

13. How regularly does Teabing fly from France to Britain to see doctors?

14. In *Deception Point*, what is the name of Senator Sedgewick Sexton's personal assistant?

15. Who receives a cellphone call and tells Langdon and Sophie that the French police have arrived at the bank?

16. Which religious group has its headquarters at 243 Lexington Avenue?

17. In *The Da Vinci Code*, who models their sleep patterns on an African warrior tribe?

18. Which of the following was the longest-serving Grand Master of the Priory of Sion: Rene D'Anjou, Nicolas Flamel or Victor Hugo?

19. Which police officer stopped Vernet and the armoured car for questioning?

20. Vernet tells the police he is driving the armoured car to where: St Thurial, St Etienne, St Tropez or St Rosalind?

21. What sum of money, in euros, had the Teacher demanded from Opus Dei?

22. Who felled Langdon to his knees, just as he was studying the writing on part of the rosewood in Teabing's house?

23. Which character in *The Da Vinci Code* had been given a cryptex during their childhood?

24. The text of Saunière's final message described what location?

25. In *Deception Point*, Senator Sexton has had an affair with which member of his staff?

26. Can you name two of the three things Fache believes fugitives always need when on the run?

27. In *Digital Fortress*, what was the name of the club at the end of the bus line in Seville that Becker went to?

28. Who in the Château Villette struck Silas where his cilice was positioned, causing him intense pain?

29. What card-based game did Sophie and her grandfather used to play: Tarot, poker or pontoon?

30. In *Deception Point*, 'Not Always Scientifically Accurate' was a sarcastic renaming of NASA published in which American newspaper?

31. Which 17th Century British scientist and author of *The Sceptical Chemist* was also a Priory of Sion Grand Master?

32. The Priory of Sion was founded in which century?

33. In *Deception Point*, the meteorite found in the Arctic weighs more than how many tonnes?

34. Orme Court is the London home of which religious organisation?

35. Who had revealed to Aringarosa the four top members of the brotherhood: Bezu Fache, Sophie Neveu, the Teacher or Robert Langdon?

36. What is the name of the hotel in which Langdon and Vittoria spend the night at the end of *Angels and Demons*?

37. In *Deception Point*, what is the name, in English, given to the method of killing which involves cramming snow down the throat of a victim?

38. What type of wine does André Vernet intend filling his cellar with once he retires?

39. According to Langdon and Teabing, who is the Holy Grail?

40. On what unlucky date in October 1307 was the start of the Church's attack on the Knights Templar and the Priory of Sion?

41. Who tells Robert Langdon in *Angels and Demons* that he has just thrown a frisbee to Nobel Prize-winner, Georges Charpak?

42. In what part of his body was King Dagobert stabbed?

43. How old was Silas when he was sent to prison: 12, 14, 16 or 18?

44. In *Deception Point*, what is Harold Brown in command of: White House security, the U.S.S. *Charlotte* or the Delta Force team in the Arctic?

45. What is the name of the BBC reporter in *Angels and Demons*?

46. In *The Da Vinci Code*, what relation was Joseph of Arimathea said to be to Jesus Christ?

47. What present did Sophie Neveu receive from her grandfather for her ninth birthday?

48. Whose fall in *Digital Fortress* caused an electrical shorting-out of Crypto's power supply?

49. Where did Langdon hide the box holding the cryptex: in a desk drawer, behind a 14th Century dresser, under a velvet-covered divan or in a medieval oak chest?

50. In *Digital Fortress*, who does Susan Fletcher discover dead, clutching a gun and with a suicide note by his side?

1. How old had Langdon been when he was given his Mickey Mouse wristwatch?

2. In *The Da Vinci Code*, who was president-general of Opus Dei?

3. How many centuries did the astrological age of Pisces last?

4. What was the name of the person who murdered Jacques Saunière?

5. When was Opus Dei founded: 1928, 1934 or 1938?

6. What type of structure in *Angels and Demons*, beginning with the letter O, was found close to the locations of the murdered cardinals?

7. Which scientist in *Deception Point* once got trapped in Antarctica and lived off seal blubber for five weeks?

8. Who was expecting to retire on a third share of 20 million euros if the Grail was found?

9. In *The Da Vinci Code*, who lived in a 17th Century estate with two lakes?

10. In *Angels and Demons*, the Hasassin took orders from a caller using what codename beginning with the letter J?

11. In *Deception Point*, what nationality was the geologist who first found the meteorite in the Arctic?

12. Where is Da Vinci's *Adoration of the Magi* held: at the Louvre, St Peter's Basilica, the Musée D'Orsay or the Uffizi?

13. To which city did Bishop Aringarosa intend to head after his meeting at Castel Gandolfo?

14. In *Digital Fortress*, who was shot with a J23 long-range stun gun?

15. Where did Sophie and Langdon abandon her SmartCar: at an embassy, a train station, a museum or a hotel?

16. In which London college had Sophie Neveu studied cryptography?

17. In *Deception Point*, who deploys a ground-penetrating radar system to test the composition of the water on the Milne Ice Shelf?

18. Which character in *Angels and Demons* had served in the military for two years but refused to fire a weapon?

19. In *The Da Vinci Code*, what does the acronym 'DCPJ' stand for?

20. What is the name of the astrological age which began at the start of the new millennium?

21. What is the first letter of the Hebrew alphabet: Alah, Amon, Alef or Atsh?

22. In *Digital Fortress*, which part of Becker's body is first hit by a bullet from Hulohot's gun: his arm, his side, his ankle or his temple?

23. In *Angels and Demons*, who hijacks a Citroen sedan using the gun lent by Commander Olivetti?

24. The Teacher instructs Rémy to park the limousine at which famous London landmark, close to St James Park?

25. In *Deception Point*, what creatures were found in the meteorite extraction shaft, leading to suspicions amongst the scientists: bacterium, plankton, isopods or sea lice?

26. Can you give either of the two reasons why Vernet does not want Langdon and Sophie to be arrested on the bank's premises?

27. How many people were in the vehicle that left Teabing's château, fleeing from the French police?

28. In *Angels and Demons*, where in Europe was Langdon first flown to?

29. Who wore a ring containing a purple amethyst and large diamonds?

30. What was the Italian word for 'left' which gave rise to the English word, 'sinister'?

31. How many passports did Teabing have in a wall-safe fitted inside his aircraft?

32. In *Digital Fortress*, Chad Brinkerhoff collected Susan at the underground highway in what sort of leisure vehicle?

33. In *Digital Fortress*, what Japanese city was the birthplace of Ensei Tankado?

34. In *The Da Vinci Code*, how long are we told Langdon's latest manuscript is: 150 pages, 300 pages, 450 pages or 750 pages?

35. In *Digital Fortress*, can you name either of the operatives sent to Spain to monitor Hulohot's activities?

36. In *Deception Point*, how many times has President Herney vetoed the space commercialization bill?

37. Which French town did Silas move to after leaving Marseilles?

38. What type of liquid is usually to be found inside the vial contained in a cryptex?

39. After Silas shoots at three police officers, who does he turn and fire upon?

40. What is the name of the nun who oversaw the non-religious running of the Church of Saint-Sulpice?

41. What is the name of the originator of *Digital Fortress*?

42. Which banker states that he had been a friend of Jacques Saunière?

43. What word, beginning the letter D, describes the volunteer guides present at Westminster Abbey?

44. Sir Leigh Teabing's third question to Langdon, while Langdon and Sophie are sitting outside Teabing's estate, is about which sport?

45. In *Deception Point*, who is the head of the National Reconnaissance Office (NRO)?

46. What was the first name of the 13th Century mathematician, Fibonacci?

47. What part of the Zurich Bank armoured car was damaged, and ground along the road as Langdon drove?

48. What colour were the heavy plastic deposit boxes in the Depository Bank of Zurich?

49. Which church was the location of the first murder of a cardinal in *Angels and Demons*: Santa Maria del Popolo, St Peter's Basilica or the Pantheon?

50. Which character in *The Da Vinci Code* had studied at the Sorbonne and has a degree in international finance?

1. Which painting was hung on the northwest wall of the Salle des Etats, protected by two inches of plexiglass?

2. Which playing card suit is derived from the Tarot card suit of Cups?

3. Who wielded the small Medusa handgun at its owner inside Temple Church?

4. Which politician in *Deception Point* had lost his wife, Katherine, in a car crash?

5. In *Angels and Demons*, the Hassassin says the first cardinal will die at what time in the evening?

6. Which North American city can boast a branch of the Depository Bank of Zurich?

7. In the Chapter House, who grabs Teabing's gun and trains it on him?

8. Who kills Rémy Legaludec?

9. According to Langdon, for how many millennia before Christ had the pentacle been used as a symbol?

10. What is the second five-letter word Sophie uses to try to open her grandfather's cryptex?

11. In *Digital Fortress*, on what part of Ensei Tankado's body were there bruises?

12. In *Deception Point*, which woman was senior advisor to President Herney?

13. What was the building number written on the back of Saunière's key?

14. What is the nickname of Rosslyn Chapel?

15. In *Angels and Demons*, who is in charge of the running of the Vatican in between popes: the camerlengo, Commander Olivetti or the Great Elector, Cardinal Mortati?

16. In which Italian city would you find the painting, *The Last Supper*?

17. What international police organisation provides the French police with details of where Robert Langdon was staying?

18. In which country's national library had proof been uncovered of famous figures as heads of the Priory of Sion?

19. In which London building did Captain Fache see Sophie Neveu for the first time since the escape from the Louvre?

20. What sort of material is the vial inside a cryptex made of?

21. In *Deception Point*, the listening-in network of 1,456 hydrophones mounted on the ocean floor is called by what name?

22. How many dollars, to the nearest ten, was Langdon carrying in his wallet when on the run in Paris?

23. In *Deception Point* what building measures just 170 feet (56 m) by 85 feet (27 m)?

24. What was the nationality of the bank for deposit-box holders that Langdon and Sophie visited?

25. In *Deception Point*, Thule Air Force Base is on the northern part of what large island?

26. Sophie and Langdon visit Temple Church on the pretence of performing what action?

27. How many words were scrawled across the glass covering the *Mona Lisa*?

28. What two letters were found embossed on the triangular-columned key which Sophie discovered when she was eight years old?

29. In *Angels and Demons*, who had been a miraculous survivor of a car-bombing tragedy in Palermo: Maximilian Kohler, Carlo Ventresca or Vittoria Vetra?

30. What is the common name of the Vatican Institute for Religious Works?

31. When does the Priory intend to release the Grail documents: in 100 years, in 500 years or never?

32. Who does the King's College librarian say is a frequent visitor and enjoys her cups of tea?

33. In *Deception Point*, what three-character password to Senator Sexton's computer did Gabrielle guess to win dinner at Davide's?

34. In *Deception Point*, from what did the Delta Force's flying micro robots derive energy?

35. What was Sophie Neveu's mother's maiden surname: Saunière, Chauvel or Fache?

36. In *Digital Fortress*, who bypassed Gauntlet to get TRANSLTR to try to crack *Digital Fortress*?

37. Who had asked the Teacher whether Silas was the right person to steal the Priory keystone from the group inside Temple Church?

38. Where were Collet and his police officers lured by Teabing's intercom system: into the study, guest bedroom II, the barn or the kitchen?

39. In *Digital Fortress*, what is the name of the portable computer Hulohot can view using special glasses given to him by the NSA deputy director?

40. Which famous Louvre artwork did Sophie Veneu find a key attached to?

41. In *Angels and Demons*, from which four countries were the four cardinals who were favourites to be elected as pope?

42. Which influential figure in *Deception Point* had lost his daughter, Diana in conflict a few years earlier?

43. What is Lieutenant Collet's first name?

44. Over which church did the Reverend Harvey Knowles preside?

45. The sarcophagus of Sir Isaac Newton's tomb is made of marble of what colour?

46. In *Deception Point*, which member of the Delta Force deploys a flash-bang to blow away the piece of ice on which Tolland, Sexton and Marlinson stand?

47. In *Angels and Demons*, which senior Swiss Guard officer was found killed in the church close to the burning bishop?

48. What female name did Teabing give to his own personal aircraft?

49. In *Angels and Demons*, what was the name given to the completely secret Illuminati meeting place towards which the Path of Illumination was supposed to lead?

50. In the painting, *The Last Supper*, what letter of the alphabet is made by the positioning of the two figures of Jesus and Mary Magdalene?

1. Which museum curator was Langdon scheduled to meet after his lecture?

2. How many dollars on his VISA card did it cost Langdon to buy the two train tickets out of Paris, as a ruse to outwit the French police?

3. In *Deception Point*, the giant meteorite was embedded underneath how many feet of ice?

4. Who discovered a hollow area underneath the floor of the Church of Saint-Sulpice?

5. In *Deception Point*, what does the acronym 'SFF' stand for?

6. How many members of the Priory of Sion know the location of the Grail at any one time?

7. In *Angels and Demons*, who is the wheelchair-bound director general of CERN?

8. Captain Fache split his forces in half – to guard the Louvre and what other set of buildings?

9. In *Deception Point*, what substance were Rachel, Tolland and Corky injected with soon after being picked up by the nuclear submarine?

10. The GPS tracking system used by the DCJP is accurate to within how many feet?

11. In *Deception Point*, how old is Gabrielle Ashe: 24, 27, 29 or 31?

12. The US Embassy stands just north of which famous Parisian thoroughfare?

13. How many million women are estimated to have been burned by the Church during three centuries of witch hunts?

14. Which Parisian building houses the Museum of Modern Art?

15. Which civilization called studying anagrams 'ars magna', meaning 'the great art'?

16. Who is the first person in *Digital Fortress* to enter the Crypto sublevels?

17. Which Bishop made the phone call to get Silas into Saint-Sulpice?

18. In *Deception Point*, who invalided Delta-Three with a Powerhead Shark Control Device?

19. What illness had Sir Leigh Teabing suffered in childhood?

20. In *Angels and Demons*, how many cardinals were missing from conclave?

21. In which country would you find approximately 2.5 million Masons?

22. In *Angels and Demons*, we are told that smoke of what colour denotes that a vote has not secured the election of a pope?

23. Who had initiated the fake meteorite project in *Deception Point*: William Pickering, Marjorie Tench or President Zach Herney?

24. In *Digital Fortress*, how long does Jabba tell Fontaine it would take for a manual shutdown of the NSA database?

25. What sort of lifelike model, designed by Da Vinci in 1495, was on Jacques Saunière's desk?

26. Who does Teabing state was given instructions by Jesus to found the Christian Church: Peter, Thomas, Constantine or Mary Magdalene?

27. Where had Silas and Aringarosa built a church together: Paris, Toulon, Madrid, Oviedo or Andorra?

28. In *Digital Fortress*, who was in charge of an NSA workstation connected to 377 phone taps and 148 CCTV cameras?

29. In *Angels and Demons*, who faxed Langdon a photograph of the dead CERN scientist and insisted he visited CERN immediately?

30. In *Deception Point*, who told NASA technicians to hide the body of Wailee Ming?

31. How many questions did Teabing ask Langdon before allowing him entrance to his château?

32. What symbol did Saunière daub on his own body as he was dying?

33. Who tries to convince Langdon and Sophie that Sophie's family were killed by the Church?

34. In *Angels and Demons*, who burns the left eye of the Hassassin shortly before he falls to his death over the balcony at the Castle of the Angel?

35. In *Deception Point*, whose wife was a school science teacher before she developed lymphoma and died?

36. What alcoholic drink does the Teacher offer Rémy to drink whilst in the limo?

37. In *Deception Point*, how many dollars was the cap on campaign donations: US$500, US$2,000, US$25,000 or US$50,000?

38. According to Bishop Aringarosa, which Biblical figure was an albino?

39. In *Angels and Demons*, how many days after the death of a pope are we told the conclave is held to elect his successor?

40. What task was the altar boy doing inside Temple Church when Teabing, Langdon and Sophie arrived?

41. In *Angels and Demons*, we are told that the Vatican City ban which of the following being visible: women's legs above the ankle, men's elbows and knees or men's and women's legs above the knee?

42. Where did the French police find a sophisticated surveillance centre: in a grotto, inside a limousine, in a hayloft or inside a private passenger aircraft?

43. Which Scottish religious building do Sophie and Langdon visit after the arrest of Sir Leigh Teabing?

44. In *Deception Point*, what two letters did Gabrielle find monogrammed on Senator Sexton's cufflinks?

45. Which French composer was the Grand Master of the Priory of Sion before Jean Cocteau and after Victor Hugo?

46. Which Tarot card suit represents the chalice?

47. In *Digital Fortress*, who aborts Susan Fletcher's tracer to determine Tankado's partner?

48. In *Angels and Demons*, whose body has Kohler preserved in a Freon cooling system?

49. Which planet traces a path across the night sky shaped like a pentacle every eight years?

50. Which of the following was a Grand Master of the Priory of Sion: Botticelli, Michelangelo or Raphael?

1. Which character in *The Da Vinci Code*, with the initials RL, was wearing a tuxedo in London?

2. What material does the Teacher use to write a message to Langdon and Sophie on the sarcophagus of Sir Isaac Newton?

3. According to *Angels and Demons*, an overdose of which substance can mimic the symptoms of a stroke and leave the victim with a black mouth?

4. Which Egyptian god had his birthday on December 25th? His name begins with the letter, O.

5. In *Angels and Demons*, in which suite were Rocio and her German client staying in: 101, 201, 301 or 401?

6. In *Deception Point*, Rachel Sexton tries to cut the weather balloon tether away with what object?

7. Who is horrified that he has become the sole remaining guardian of the secret of the Priory?

8. In *Deception Point*, who loses their goggles due to the ice collapse: Rachel, Tolland or Corky?

9.   How many advance copies of Langdon's latest book manuscript did his editor send out to experts in the art world?

10. How many of the sénéchaux confirmed to Silas that the keystone existed: none, one or all?

11. In *Digital Fortress*, what did the simple coded message, LD SNN, written by Becker to Fletcher, stand for?

12. Who had placed the GPS tracking dot on Langdon?

13. In *Deception Point*, what was the name given to the figure who commanded the Delta Force team?

14. What letter is used for the legendary document alleged to be about Jesus's teachings and possibly written by him?

15. The cult of Sol Invictus was a popular religion from which civilization: Ancient Rome, Ancient Greece or Ancient Egypt?

16. Which two-word surname was one of the two family names of the direct descendents of the Merovingians?

17. In *Digital Fortress*, how many million processors did TRANSLTR have running together?

18. In *Deception Point*, after Rachel Sexton was picked up by the nuclear submarine, whom did she ask to speak to first?

19. In *Digital Fortress*, what does NSA stand for?

20. How wide is the *Mona Lisa* painting, to the nearest four inches?

21. In *Angels and Demons*, who is a strict vegetarian and a hatha yoga expert: Maximilian Kohler, Vittoria Vetra or Jacqui Tomaso?

22. In *Digital Fortress*, with whom is Brinkerhoff having an affair with: Rocio, Carmen or Susan?

23. By what ancient Egyptian-inspired nickname was President Mitterrand sometimes known?

24. How many panes of glass is the Louvre pyramid made from: 99, 101, 666 or 1149?

25. The god, Baphomet, was commonly portrayed as having the head of which animal: a ram, a pig, a bull or a lioness?

26. In *Angels and Demons*, who was killed by Swiss Guard bullets as he held a gun at the camerlengo in the Pope's Office?

27. In *The Da Vinci Code*, how long has it been since Langdon had seen Vittoria: a month, three month, sixth months or over a year?

28. The famous parquet flooring of the Louvre's Grand Gallery is made from what type of wood: oak, ash, rosewood or mahogany?

29. In *Angels and Demons*, antimatter's chemical signature is equivalent to which element: hydrogen, carbon, mercury or antimony?

30. Teabing's plane landed at which English airfield?

31. In *Deception Point*, who uses duct tape to cover his leg wound?

32. Which finger did Jacques Saunière's dip in his own gunshot wound to use as a pen?

33. In *Deception Point*, who carries a sample of the meteorite with them after their escape?

34. In *Angels and Demons*, how old was Cardinal Mortati, the eldest cardinal in the Vatican conclave?

35. When Langdon entered Teabing's château, what item of clothing did he wrap around the rosewood box to hide it from view?

36. In *Digital Fortress*, Becker first hoped to meet Rocio and her German client in which hotel: the Alfonso XIII, the General Cesare or the Principe?

37. In *Deception Point*, which politician wore bifocal glasses, had thinning black hair and met Rachel Sexton wearing hiking boots?

38. In which building were Langdon and Sophie surprised to discover Sir Leigh Teabing pointing a gun at them?

39. The Garden of Earthly Pleasures was part of a park found where: in Milan, Rome, New York or Paris?

40. Who does the Teacher instruct to enter Teabing's château to steal the cryptex?

41. Robert Langdon had once given a lecture on Da Vinci at the National Gallery – in which city?

42. Which book about the Holy Grail does Teabing show Sophie, stating that it was a bestseller in the 1980s?

43. According to Teabing, whose tomb must the Priory of Sion protect?

44. In *Digital Fortress*, what is the five-character password with which Fletcher opens Strathmore's elevator?

45. In *Deception Point*, how many civilian scientists has President Herney sent to the Arctic to confirm NASA's findings?

46. Who had expressed interest to Jacques Saunière in funding a new Da Vinci wing of the Louvre Museum?

47. In *Angels and Demons*, which saint was crucified upside down and buried five storeys below ground?

48. Who carried the Medusa revolver into Westminster Abbey?

49. How long did the Vatican give Opus Dei to voluntarily break away and become its own church?

50. In *Deception Point*, what did Tolland unfurl out on the ice to escape from Delta Force: a weather balloon, a yacht sail or a giant flag?

1. How many bullets were fired into Jacques Saunière's body?

2. According to *Deception Point*, the Roswell Incident was an accident during which classified spy balloon project, beginning with the letter M?

3. Who carried a Heckler and Koch handgun into the Church of Saint-Sulpice?

4. In *Angels and Demons*, what was Robert Langdon given from the papal vault, on indefinite loan?

5. In *Deception Point*, Ralph Sneeden is a reporter with which major US newspaper?

6. In *The Da Vinci Code*, who braves airsickness to fly in a Beechcraft Baron light aircraft to London?

7. Where had the GPS tracking device been placed on Langdon: at the Hotel Ritz, in the police car or at the Louvre?

8. In *Angels and Demons*, what item did Robert Langdon grab from the helicopter to help provide drag before jumping out?

9. Who hits Teabing in the back and then appears to take him hostage in return for the keystone?

10. How long had Saunière been a curator at the Louvre: 20 years, 35 years, 50 years or 55 years?

11. The Depository Bank of Zurich's gold accounts lease deposit boxes for a minimum of how many years: five, 25, 50, 100 or 250?

12. In *Angels and Demons*, who was the second corpse found with their head turned 180 degrees backward?

13. When Langdon arrives at the Louvre, which major wing does Fache guide him through first?

14. In *Digital Fortress*, David Becker obtains Tankado's ring outside a terminal at which airport?

15. Who was the Egyptian god of masculine fertility: Amon, Osiris or Isis?

16. Which character in *Digital Fortress* drives a white Lotus equipped with all manner of gadgets?

17. In *Deception Point*, Space Industries of Houston have proposed to build a space station for how much money: $5 billion, $15 billion or $35 billion?

18. Which king established King's College in London: King James I, King George IV, King Edward VII or King William III?

19. We are told in *Angels and Demons*, that an applicant to join the Swiss Guards has to be under what age?

20. In which European city, beginning with the letter F, was the stolen *Mona Lisa* discovered in a hotel room?

21. In *Deception Point*, who was asked by President Herney to go to the Arctic to make a 15-minute documentary on the meteorite discovery?

22. By what name, beginning with the letter, B, is the Priory of Sion also known?

23. In *Angels and Demons*, what word means 'enlightened ones'?

24. In *Digital Fortress*, who is Trevor Strathmore in love with?

25. According to Teabing, how many trunks hold the Holy Grail documents?

26. In *Angels and Demons*, what nationality was the controller of the media truck whose crane Langdon used to get into the Castle of the Angel?

27. What three words were the mantra of Father Josemaría Escrivá?

28. In *Digital Fortress*, what is the first name of the punk girl Becker is searching for in Seville?

29. How many Priory of Sion Grand Masters had been women?

30. Who, apart from her mother and father, had Sophie believed died in the car crash when she was just a young child?

31. In *Digital Fortress*, who turned out to be ordering the assassin, Hulohot?

32. In *Angels and Demons*, how many miles up did the pilot of the prototype Boeing X-33 tell Langdon his craft would fly if heading for Tokyo?

33. In the 14th Century, the Priory of Sion's secret documents were moved in secret by a ship sailing from where: Calais, Biarritz, La Rochelle or Copenhagen?

34. In *The Da Vinci Code*, what position did Michael Breton hold: chief curator at the Mitterand Library, senior archivist at King's College or head of French Intelligence?

35. What item did Silas use to kill Sister Sandrine?

36. Which of the four cardinals in *Angels and Demons* was the last to be murdered?

37. In *Digital Fortress*, how many pesetas did David Becker pay Rafael de la Maza for a black blazer?

38. In what country had Silas spent a long time in prison: France, Spain, Italy or Andorra?

39. In *Digital Fortress*, when Langdon is trying to save the first cardinal, to which famous ancient Roman building does he mistakenly lead the Swiss Guard?

40. What colour was the Ferrari in Teabing's sports car collection?

41. In *Digital Fortress*, where was Megan seeking a plane flight to: Miami, Tokyo, Connecticut or Washington?

42. Who bought a present of Chinese kissing fish and a bunch of white lilies at the end of *Deception Point*?

43. After Silas left home, he lived on the streets of which French city?

44. Who deciphered the verse written on the wooden rose from Saunière's box?

45. What Biblical name was discovered on the stone Silas unearthed from Saint-Sulpice?

46. In *Deception Point*, what was the name of the laser-guided missile fitted to the Delta Force helicopter?

47. In *Digital Fortress*, which punk's neck was broken shortly after he talked to David Becker?

48. Where was the British police going to take Bishop Aringarosa before he insisted on a detour to the London Opus Dei centre?

49. Who used a small ultraviolet torch from the French police forensics to search for a message from Jacques Saunière?

50. In *Deception Point*, what word, beginning with the letter G, described Rachel Sexton's job of analysing reports to prepare short, clear briefs?

UNBREAKABLE QUIZ

1. How many times had Langdon been denied access to the Vatican Archives?

2. Which of Paris's art museums, viewable from the Tuileries Gardens, is marked by a large, ancient Egyptian obelisk?

3. In *Digital Fortress*, what is the name of the tourist that Becker questioned inside the Seville clinic?

4. In *Deception Point*, what three words described the outer surface of the meteorite?

5. What is the name of the giant stone archway in the Tuileries Gardens in Paris?

6. In *Digital Fortress*, what is the name of the cardinal who shows Becker the curtained secret door out of the cathedral?

7. Langdon's lecture in Paris was about the hidden symbols in the stones of which French cathedral?

8. In *Digital Fortress*, what was the name of the terrorist plan that was to use magnetic fields to wipe the electronic equipment at the New York Stock Exchange?

9. At which educational institution in France had Robert Langdon given a lecture?

10. How old is the Arctic meteorite in *Deception Point*, to the nearest ten million years?

11. In *Digital Fortress*, what is the name of the director of the NSA's personal aide?

12. From which chapter of the Bible did Silas take his name?

13. In *Digital Fortress*, what was the name of the man Hulohot killed in Seville Cathedral?

14. What was the draft title of Langdon's manuscript in *The Da Vinci Code*?

15. According to *Deception Point*, arthropoda – the phylum which contain insects – make up what percentage of all species on Earth?

16. What was the name of the security warden who caught Langdon and Neveu near the *Mona Lisa*?

17. In *Deception Point*, what was the name of the updatable index of marine species used by Tolland to locate the giant fossil louse?

18. In the number sequence Jacques Saunière wrote in the Louvre using a watermark stylus, what was the largest of the numbers?

19. In *The Da Vinci Code*, what was the first name of the hostess of Langdon's Paris lecture?

20. In *Angels and Demons*, what was the number of the security camera which was focused on the canister of antimatter?

21. In *Digital Fortress*, what nationality was the author of the 1987 paper on rotating cleartext?

22. In *Angels and Demons*, what was the estimated value of the Vatican City, to the nearest half a billion US dollars?

23. Which documents were found in 1975 that identified many members of the Priory of Sion?

24. In *Angels and Demons*, what amount of antimatter had been stolen from the Haz-Mat Chamber at CERN?

25. In *Digital Fortress*, what was the name of the new crossbreed computer language that Susan Fletcher wrote the tracer in?

26. What was the last word in the third line of the message Saunière wrote close to his body using the watermark stylus?

27. In *Deception Point*, who was the first to call the President of the United States from a Portable Secure Communications (PSC) booth?

28. How long is the Louvre's Grand Gallery, to the nearest hundred feet?

29. What does 'ODAN' stand for in *The Da Vinci Code*?

30. What is the name of the real-life FBI spy who, in *The Da Vinci Code*, is labelled a prominent member of Opus Dei?

31. In *Digital Fortress*, 'Big Brother' is a Centrex 333 computer connected to how many electronic doors?

32. Who did Silas refer to as 'the Teacher of all Teachers'?

33. In *Deception Point*, in which deep ocean location had the meteorite originally been found by the NRO?

34. In *Angels and Demons*, which Italian cardinal was expected to win the election to be pope, but was murdered?

35. Paris fire codes insist on windows above a certain height being breakable. What height is this (in metres)?

36. In *Digital Fortress*, what is the error code number for a manual abort in Node 3?

37. Can you name either of the two notorious Frenchmen who were baptised at Saint-Sulpice?

38. Which verse of Chapter 38 of the Book of Job did Silas read after discovering the stone at Saint-Sulpice?

39. In *Angels and Demons*, after the Hassassin kills, he flicks through a book of sexual escorts. What is the name of the Japanese geisha girl on offer?

40. By what name do the French call *Mona Lisa*?

41. In *Digital Fortress*, what is the name of the German client of the escort shot dead by Hulohot?

42. In *Angels and Demons*, what is the name of the particle accelerator at CERN which the Vetras used for their antimatter experiments?

43. In *Deception Point*, how many SWATH design ships had been made other than the *Goya*?

44. How many bronze markers denote the north to south Rose Line that runs through Paris?

45. In *Digital Fortress*, how many flights of steps into the Crypto sublevels had Susan Fletcher descended before she heard a gunshot above?

46. In *Deception Point*, which aircraft piloted by Delta Force operatives is capable of travelling at speeds in excess of Mach 6?

47. What was the name of the Council which Teabing said voted to create Jesus a god not a mortal?

48. After Langdon appeared on a TV programme about the Grail, the Catholic bishop of which American city sent him a critical postcard?

49. In *Digital Fortress*, what was the nickname of the flight that Megan hoped to take from Spain across the Atlantic?

50. Can you recall the precise ten-digit code used by Langdon and Neveu at the Depository Bank to gain access to the cryptex?

EASY ACCESS
ANSWERS

1. The Louvre
2. Robert Langdon
3. Sophie Neveu
4. Sir Leigh Teabing
5. Arctic
6. Silas
7. American
8. Hearing
9. Michael Tolland
10. Robert Langdon

11. A French accent
12. *Deception Point*
13. Paris
14. Zach Herney
15. Opus Dei
16. Jabba
17. Cryptex
18. Washington
19. Versailles
20. Bezu Fache

21. Harvard
22. David Becker
23. Paris
24. Vittoria Vetra
25. Harry Houdini

26. An American eagle
27. Vatican City
28. His right
29. Rachel Sexton
30. A dove

31. Holy Grail
32. Sir Leigh Teabing
33. Illuminati
34. The Atlantic
35. New York
36. Sedgewick Sexton
37. Silas
38. On a moped
39. Rome
40. Sophie Neveu

41. A punk
42. Rémy Legaludec
43. Rome
44. Bill Gates
45. Fleet Street
46. Robert Langdon
47. Captain Fache
48. South America
49. Barcelona
50. Walt Disney

CRYPTIC AND MYSTIC ANSWERS

QUIZ 1

1. Jesus Christ
2. Lille
3. Robert Langdon
4. 13
5. Uriel
6. A cilice
7. 24 hour countdown
8. Seven
9. Atbash Cipher
10. Westminster Abbey

11. Canadian
12. Alitalia
13. Top Secret Umbra
14. Florence
15. An iron cross
16. 60 cm (two feet)
17. Delius's
18. David Becker
19. Silas's
20. Tankado

21. The Purdue Hotel
22. A candle pole
23. Hammerhead shark
24. Robert Langdon
25. Th
26. Ground-penetrating radar
27. Greg Hale's

28. Marjorie Tench
29. 5 million
30. Two hours

31. Oxford University
32. A fake name Rachel Sexton gave to buy time
33. Paris
34. Panspermia
35. Sophie Neveu
36. Polar Orbiting Density Scanner
37. The Swiss Guards
38. An armoured car
39. A human skull
40. Sir Leigh Teabing

41. Maximilian Kohler
42. Octagonal
43. British *Tatler*
44. Boeing 747
45. The United Nations Building
46. Brass
47. Josemaría Escrivá
48. Sir Leigh Teabing's
49. Emergency Transponder
50. Silas

QUIZ 2

1. Black
2. The altar boy
3. One square yard
4. Jacques Saunière
5. Portuguese
6. Two
7. The British flag
8. Lawrence Ekstrom
9. Silas
10. Robert Langdon

11. Galileo Galilei
12. 12 years
13. Marjorie Tench
14. Barcodes
15. The Pole
16. Three feet
17. English
18. The French police
19. Marie Chauvel
20. Bev (Beverley)

21. A GPS tracking dot
22. Leland Fontaine
23. English
24. Sofia
25. André Vernet
26. The Illuminati Diamond
27. Two Tone
28. The camerlengo (Carlo Ventresca)

29. Planets
30. The Quaker

31. Milan
32. Maximilian Kohler
33. Earth Observation System
34. US Embassy
35. The *Goya*
36. Plantard
37. *Julius Caesar*
38. A Delta Force helicopter
39. Sophie Neveu
40. The Apprentice Pillar, the Mason's Pillar

41. Strathmore's
42. Dabbling in technology stocks
43. Who will guard the guards?
44. The BBC
45. 200 tonnes
46. David Becker
47. Sexton
48. *The Last Supper*
49. CERN
50. Jesus, the Virgin Mary, John the Baptist, Angel Uriel

QUIZ 3

1. Saint-Sulpice
2. Robert Langdon
3. Constantine
4. Greg Hale
5. Captain Bezu Fache
6. $10,000
7. U.S.S. *Charlotte*
8. Bishop Aringarosa
9. Gabrielle Ashe
10. Richard

11. His right leg
12. 13
13. Lieutenant Collet
14. November
15. 18
16. Her brother
17. 26,000
18. Sandro Botticelli
19. Jacques Saunière
20. Global Hawk

21. Taxi
22. Wailee Ming
23. An earthquake
24. France
25. Hexagonal

26. A tapestry
27. Corky Marlinson
28. Camerlengo Ventresca
29. The Lincoln Bedroom
30. L'Isa

31. 100 km
32. King's College, London
33. Egyptian
34. Red
35. Manuel
36. A clay pit
37. Black
38. A knotted rope
39. Princess Sophie
40. The Mitterrand Library

41. Norah Mangor
42. Captain Fache
43. Thomas
44. Castel Gandolfo
45. Node 3
46. eight
47. Vittoria Vetra
48. 10 years
49. National Gallery, London
50. Krishna

QUIZ 4

1. His shoulder
2. Rachel Sexton
3. Bishop Aringarosa
4. The Holy Grail
5. A paper clip
6. Leonardo da Vinci
7. A bullet cartridge
8. The Grand Gallery
9. Gabrielle Ashe
10. Switzerland and France

11. A key
12. Female bees
13. A cross
14. The 18th Century
15. The Hebrew alphabet
16. Silas
17. His elbow
18. King Phillipe IV
19. Physicist
20. King Baldwin II

21. 12th Century
22. Isis
23. Leland Fontaine
24. 27 km
25. Cardinal Guidera

26. Castel Gandolfo
27. Maryland
28. Leather
29. Off and die
30. Water polo

31. Vernet
32. 63
33. Cardinal Baggia
34. The Coast Guard
35. Robert Langdon
36. Chris Harper
37. Bishop Aringarosa
38. Dr Mangor
39. Bezu Fache
40. A petrol leak

41. Six storeys
42. Westminster Abbey
43. Lieutenant Chartrand
44. The Teacher
45. Cardinal Ebner
46. Ensei Tankado
47. Sir Leigh Teabing
48. Leonardo da Vinci
49. The third cardinal
50. His body

QUIZ 5

1. Sarah
2. Jabba
3. 15 years ago
4. A cross
5. The Teacher
6. Xavia
7. The preferiti
8. To torture
9. Halite
10. A mysterious key

11. Secretarius Vaticana
12. The Sistine Chapel
13. Royal Blood
14. Rémy Legaludec
15. More than 140
16. US$47 million
17. Vittoria Vetra
18. *The Gravity of Genius*
19. Weeding the garden
20. Sir Leigh Teabing

21. The Wind Rose
22. Captain Fache
23. Skydiving
24. Silver
25. Robert Langdon
26. 25th December

27. Robert Langdon, Sophie Neveu
28. Camerlengo Ventresca
29. 10
30. Vittoria Vetra

31. Georgetown University
22. The Illuminati
33. Three
34. Three
35. Sfumato
36. The spring equinox
37. Maximilian Kohler
38. Greg Hale
39. A ring
40. Black light

41. Georges Lemaître
42. They were pushed out of a helicopter
43. The late Pope
44. The chalice
45. André (Vernet)
46. PODS
47. The Little Passage, Il Passetto
48. Five
49. Corky Marlinson
50. Rome

QUIZ 6

1. God's Work
2. Commander Strathmore
3. One centimetre
4. Francois Mitterrand
5. Sir Leigh Teabing
6. Charles Brophy
7. Blue
8. Silas
9. Jabba
10. Red

11. Temple
12. Fiat
13. The third floor
14. Sophie Neveu
15. Trevor
16. Rachel Sexton
17. Her duffel bag
18. 22
19. *Boston* magazine
20. Florence

21. Highway 5
22. Saunière
23. Greg Hale
24. Chinita Macri
25. A mile away
26. The Louvre
27. Stradivarius
28. Sir Leigh Teabing

29. POTUS (President of the United States)
30. The Star of David
31. The Rose Line
32. In the bottom drawer of his dresser
33. Temple Church
34. Rémy Legaludec
35. Golden coloured shoes
36. Bernini
37. André Vernet
38. Venus, Jesus, Maria, Greal, Sarah, Grail, Graal
39. Red
40. A canvas mat

41. Leonardo Da Vinci
42. His grandmother
43. $31 million ($30.8 million)
44. 13
45. Apple
46. English, French and German
47. André Vernet
48. A handgun
49. The sénéchaux
50. Temple Church

QUIZ 7

1. Poseidon
2. William Pickering
3. Swords, pentacles, cups, sceptres
4. Salle des Etats
5. American Remailers Anonymous
6. St Mary's Hospital
7. Castle of the Angel
8. Platinum
9. Saliva
10. Maximilian Kohler

11. Commander Strathmore
12. A stroke
13. The Coptic Scrolls
14. Roland Garros
15. Vellum
16. A Hawker 731
17. Lieutenant Collet
18. A vodka
19. The Swiss Guard
20. 12

21. Three
22. Purple
23. Santa Cruz
24. The Hindu religion

25. Bishop Aringarosa
26. Avenue Gabriel
27. Collet
28. Robert Langdon
29. Jonas Faukman
30. Greg Hale

31. A one dollar bill
32. A micro robot
33. Knight, London, Pope
34. Robert Langdon
35. Origins
36. Red
37. *Deception Point*
38. Susan
39. Spain
40. The Louvre

41. The Arc de Triomphe
42. Susan Fletcher
43. 1 am
44. Jacques Saunière's office
45. His toe
46. London
47. The Musée d'Orsay
48. Captain Fache
49. Harvard University
50. Leigh Teabing

QUIZ 8

1. Sophie Neveu
2. Kuala Lumpur
3. The altar boy
4. Sir Leigh Teabing
5. A helicopter
6. A 32-degree Mason
7. Saturday
8. French and English
9. Commander Strathmore
10. Robert Langdon

11. The toilet
12. Leland Fontaine
13. Senator Sedgewick Sexton
14. Aurora
15. Mars
16. The Controller
17. Over 60,000
18. A gnomon
19. Norah Mangor
20. Internal security analyst

21. Seven
22. A bank
23. A Jaguar
24. Mary Magdalene
25. Paris

26. Greek
27. Tuesday
28. His cloak
29. The 1950s
30. Rémy Legaludec

31. Yolanda Cole
32. A Volvo
33. The families of those whom Silas murdered
34. The Sully Wing
35. The Church
36. Musée du Jeu de Paume
37. A gel
38. Robert Langdon
39. *The Way*
40. Jabba

41. Jacques Saunière
42. Digital Fortress
43. Leonardo da Vinci
44. Edinburgh
45. *Angels and Demons*
46. An obelisk
47. The lefthand side
48. An F-14 Tomcat
49. Robert Langdon
50. Two

QUIZ 9

1. Bishop Aringarosa
2. Horus
3. Over half
4. 26
5. Simon Edwards
6. The Knights Templar
7. Six hours
8. Womb
9. Three
10. Solomon's Temple

11. Single
12. Grail
13. Lieutenant
14. The Teacher
15. Number 27
16. 35 years
17. Vault 10
18. Captain Fache
19. Wallops Island
20. Seven languages

21. Isis
22. The *Mona Lisa*
23. Sister Sandrine Bieil
24. Commander Strathmore
25. The Teacher
26. David Becker

27. An isopod
28. The French soccer team
29. Cardinal Mortati
30. Brainstorm

31. *Amazing Seas*
32. Judas Taboo
33. 50
34. Bezu Fache
35. The Musée d'Orsay
36. Dr Wailee Ming
37. Man
38. Robert Langdon
39. The NRO (National Reconnaissance Office)
40. Robert Langdon

41. Sofia
42. US$15 billion
43. 503
44. £2,000
45. Rosewood
46. One
47. A Rolex
48. Jerusalem
49. Leonardo Vetra
50. The Caesar Box

QUIZ 10

1. Crux gemmata
2. 1911
3. Robert Langdon
4. Sophie Neveu
5. Cardinal Ebner
6. Papyrus
7. Tokugen Numataka
8. Leonardo da Vinci
9. The NSA command centre
10. Robert Langdon

11. The lily
12. Canadian
13. Captain Fache
14. Norah Mangor
15. Egypt
16. Kensington Gardens
17. Zirconium content
18. Marble
19. 20,000
20. Sun worship

21. Rosslyn Chapel
22. Police Technical et Scientifique
23. Commander Olivetti
24. Normandy
25. French

26. Sir Isaac Newton
27. Cryptography
28. Yes
29. His right wrist
30. Pope Innocent II

31. Lawrence Ekstrom
32. The nave
33. Portuguese man-o'-wars
34. Her grandfather
35. Anyone holding them could cash them in
36. Five
37. The Dolphin
38. CERN's Haz-Mat Chamber
39. Louvre Lite
40. King's College

41. Captain Elias Rocher
42. Jacques Saunière
43. Mach 15 flight
44. Fleur-de-lis
45. Ronnie's Rumpus Room
46. Dr Jacobus
47. Female
48. Tea
49. Cardinal Baggia
50. A case of ham

QUIZ 11

1. The Louvre
2. April
3. One
4. Venus
5. Marjorie Tench
6. The Great Redeemer
7. Duct tape
8. Eighth
9. Four
10. The Ganges, Danube, Rio Plata, Nile

11. Never married
12. $1,900 million
13. A fighter jet
14. Earth
15. 454
16. Dark
17. France's
18. Sophie Neveu
19. Six
20. The NRO

21. Blue, gold
22. Beretta
23. The Grand Gallery
24. Blue
25. The Washington Monument

26. Number three
27. Alfa-Romeo
28. Tennis
29. 76
30. $300

31. 22
32. Robert Langdon
33. Interpol
34. Dagobert
35. 10 billion
36. 1.618
37. Gunter Glick
38. France (then known as Gaul)
39. Four
40. Earth, air, fire, water

41. Robert Langdon
42. Fache
43. Silas
44. The Louvre
45. Delta-Three
46. William the Conqueror
47. A tramp
48. Opus Dei
49. Bishop Aringarosa
50. Commander Strathmore

QUIZ 12

1. Mary Magdalene
2. Midnight
3. A dagger
4. The Depository Bank of Zurich
5. Norah Mangor
6. Crimson
7. Five
8. A bar of soap
9. Corky Marlinson
10. College Garden

11. The Hotel Ritz
12. A lily
13. Latin
14. Five
15. Amon
16. The altar boy
17. One
18. Porsche, Rolls Royce, Ferrari, Range Rover, Aston Martin, Daimler
19. Sophie
20. A book

21. The feminine side of the world
22. Babel
23. Chinita Macri
24. Robert Langdon and Sophie Neveu

25. A cup or chalice
26. Phil Chartrukian's
27. *Air Force One*
28. Red
29. The London Eye
30. Father Mangano

31. La Petite Versailles
32. Rémy Legaludec
33. David Becker
34. The immediate right
35. Rémy Legaludec
36. A mirror
37. Kelly Horan-Jones
38. Leonardo da Vinci International Airport
39. A Range Rover
40. Gunter Glick

41. A rose
42. Sir Leigh Teabing
43. The ballroom
44. A rose
45. Marjorie Tench
46. Three
47. Pamela Gettum
48. His eye
49. An Audi
50. Two (Robert Boyle and Robert Fludd)

QUIZ 13

1. Captain Fache
2. Commander Strathmore
3. Jacques Saunière
4. Le Bourget
5. Bishop Aringarosa
6. Michael Tolland
7. A Saab 900
8. An orb
9. 1447
10. Both leg braces and crutches

11. Three
12. Sir Isaac Newton
13. 10
14. It doubled in speed
15. *The Hunchback of Nôtre Dame*
16. 12 million
17. Nine
18. The camerlengo (Carlo Ventresca)
19. 1975
20. Michelangelo

21. The River Tiber
22. Château Villette
23. His shoes
24. The Dead Room
25. 1.6

26. Kistler Aerospace, Beal Aerospace, Space America, Microcosm, Rotary Rocket Company
27. Sophie Neveu
28. Rémy Legaludec
29. Commander Strathmore
30. His eye

31. Solomon's Temple
32. President Truman
33. Peter
34. Her grandmother and her brother
35. Nancy Reagan
36. Kent
37. 71 feet
38. *The Vitruvian Man*
39. Scones
40. André Vernet

41. A tennis ball can
42. Marjorie Tench
43. The Louvre
44. More than 80
45. 34
46. Constantine
47. Jacques Saunière
48. Wailee Ming
49. Gianlorenzo Bernini
50. Captain Fache

QUIZ 14

1. The model medieval knight
2. Chondrules
3. The founder of the Priory of Sion
4. The second cardinal
5. Delta-Two
6. The Gospel of Philip
7. Saint-Sulpice
8. PHI
9. Her father (Senator Sexton)
10. Jean Cocteau

11. His nose
12. £50 notes
13. Fortnightly
14. Gabrielle Ashe
15. André Vernet
16. Opus Dei
17. André Vernet
18. Rene D'Anjou
19. Lieutenant Collet
20. St Thurial

21. 20 million euros
22. Silas
23. Sophie Neveu
24. Roslin (Rosslyn)

25. Gabrielle Ashe
26. Cash, travel, lodging
27. Club Embrujo
28. Sir Leigh Teabing
29. Tarot
30. The *New York Times*

31. Robert Boyle
32. 11th Century
33. Eight
34. Opus Dei
35. The Teacher
36. Hotel Bernini
37. White Death
38. Bordeaux
39. Mary Magdalene
40. Friday 13th

41. Maximilian Kohler
42. His eye
43. 18
44. The U.S.S. *Charlotte*
45. Gunter Glick
46. His uncle
47. A red bicycle
48. Phil Chartrukian
49. Under a velvet-covered divan
50. Greg Hale

QUIZ 15

1. 10
2. Bishop Aringarosa
3. 20 centuries
4. Silas
5. 1928
6. Obelisk
7. Dr Norah Mangor
8. Rémy Legaludec
9. Sir Leigh Teabing
10. Janus

11. Canadian
12. The Uffizi
13. Paris
14. David Becker
15. A train station
16. Royal Holloway
17. Norah Mangor
18. Camerlengo Ventresca
19. Direction Centrale Police Judiciare
20. Age of Aquarius

21. Alef
22. His side
23. Robert Langdon
24. Horse Guards Parade
25. Plankton
26. Bad publicity for the bank, Saunière was a friend

27. Five
28. Geneva, Switzerland
29. Bishop Aringarosa
30. Sinistra

31. Two
32. A golf cart
33. Hiroshima
34. 300 pages
35. Agent Coliander, Agent Smith
36. Twice
37. Toulon
38. Vinegar
39. Bishop Aringarosa
40. Sister Sandrine Bieil

41. Ensei Tankado
42. André Vernet
43. Docents
44. Rowing
45. William Pickering
46. Leonardo
47. The front bumper
48. Black
49. Santa Maria del Popolo
50. André Vernet

QUIZ 16

1. The *Mona Lisa*
2. Hearts
3. Rémy Legaludec
4. Senator Sedgewick Sexton
5. 8 o'clock
6. New York
7. Sophie Neveu
8. The Teacher
9. Four
10. Vinci

11. Chest
12. Marjorie Tench
13. 24
14. The Cathedral of Codes
15. The camerlengo
16. Milan
17. Interpol
18. France
19. Chapter House
20. Glass

21. Classic Wizard
22. $100
23. The White House
24. Swiss
25. Greenland
26. Scattering ashes

27. Six
28. PS
29. Carlo Ventresca
30. The Vatican Bank

31. Never
32. Sir Leigh Teabing
33. SSS
34. Magnetic fields
35. Chauvel
36. Commander Strathmore
37. Rémy Legaludec
38. Guest bedroom II
39. Monocle
40. The *Mona Lisa*

41. Spain, Italy, France and Germany
42. William Pickering
43. Jerôme
44. Temple Church
45. Black marble
46. Delta-One
47. Commander Olivetti
48. Elizabeth
49. The Church Of Illumination
50. The letter M

QUIZ 17

1. Jacques Saunière
2. $70
3. 200 feet
4. Silas
5. Space Frontier Foundation
6. Four
7. Maximilian Kohler
8. The US Embassy
9. Adrenaline
10. To within two feet

11. 24
12. The Champs-Elysées
13. Five million
14. The Pompidou Centre
15. The Romans
16. Phil Chartrukian
17. Bishop Aringarosa
18. Michael Tolland
19. Polio
20. Four

21. The United States
22. Black
23. William Pickering
24. 30 minutes
25. A medieval knight
26. Mary Magdalene

27. Oviedo
28. Midge Milken
29. Maximilian Kohler
30. Lawrence Ekstrom (NASA administrator)
31. Three
32. A pentacle
33. Sir Leigh Teabing
34. Vittoria Vetra
35. Michael Tolland's
36. Cognac brandy
37. US$2,000
38. Noah
39. 15 days
40. Vacuuming

41. Men's and women's legs above the knee
42. In a hayloft
43. Rosslyn Chapel
44. SS
45. Claude Debussy
46. Cups
47. Greg Hale
48. Leonardo Vetra
49. Venus
50. Botticelli

QUIZ 18

1. Rémy Legaludec
2. Charcoal
3. Heparin
4. Osiris
5. Suite 301
6. An ice axe
7. Jacques Saunière
8. Rachel
9. 10
10. All

11. Me too
12. Lieutenant Collet
13. The Controller
14. The Q Document
15. Ancient Rome
16. Saint-Clair
17. 3 million
18. William Pickering
19. National Security Agency
20. 21 inches

21. Vittoria Vetra
22. Carmen
23. The Sphinx
24. 666
25. A ram
26. Maximilian Kohler

27. Over a year
28. Oak
29. Hydrogen
30. Biggin Hill

31. Corky Marlinson
32. His left index finger
33. Corky Marlinson
34. 79
35. His jacket
36. The Alfonso XIII
37. President Herney
38. Chapter House
39. Paris
40. Silas

41. London
42. *Holy Blood, Holy Grail*
43. The tomb of Mary
   Magdalene
44. Susan
45. Four
46. Sir Leigh Teabing
47. St Peter
48. Leigh Teabing
49. Six months
50. A weather balloon

QUIZ 19

1. One
2. Project Mogul
3. Silas
4. The Illuminati Diamond
5. The *Washington Post*
6. Bishop Aringarosa
7. The Hotel Ritz
8. The windscreen tarpaulin
9. Rémy Legaludec
10. 20 years

11. 50 years
12. Olivetti
13. The Denon Wing
14. Seville
15. Amon
16. Greg Hale
17. $5 billion
18. King George IV
19. Under 30
20. Florence

21. Michael Tolland
22. The Brotherhood
23. Illuminati
24. Susan Fletcher
25. Four
26. Australian

27. Pain is good
28. Megan
29. Four
30. Her brother and her grandmother

31. Commander Strathmore
32. 100 miles
33. La Rochelle
34. Head of French Intelligence
35. A candle-holder
36. Cardinal Baggia
37. 50,000 pesetas
38. Andorra
39. The Pantheon
40. Black

41. Connecticut
42. Michael Tolland
43. Marseilles
44. Sophie
45. Job
46. Hellfire
47. Two Tone
48. Scotland Yard
49. Sophie Neveu
50. Gisting

UNBREAKABLE ANSWERS

1. Seven
2. Musée du Jeu de Paume
3. Pierre Cloucharde
4. Charred fusion crust
5. Arc du Carrousel
6. Cardinal Guerra
7. Chartres
8. Sherwood Forest
9. The American University of Paris
10. 190 million years

11. Chad Brinkerhoff
12. Acts 16
13. Rafael de la Maza
14. *Symbols of the Lost Sacred Feminine*
15. 95%
16. Claude Grouard
17. Project Diversitas
18. 21
19. Monique
20. Number 86

21. Hungarian
22. $48.5 billion
23. Les Dossiers Secrets
24. One quarter of a gram
25. LIMBO

26. Saint
27. Rachel Sexton
28. 1,500 feet
29. Opus Dei Awareness Network
30. Robert Hanssen

31. 399
32. Father Josemaría Escrivá
33. The Mariana Trench
34. Cardinal Aldo Baggia
35. 15 metres
36. Error Code 22
37. Baudelaire and the Marquis de Sade
38. Verse 11
39. Sachiko
40. La Joconde

41. Hans Huber
42. Large Hadron Collider
43. 16
44. 135
45. Six
46. *Aurora*
47. The Council of Nicaea
48. Philadelphia
49. The Roach Coach
50. 1123581321